Mel Bay Presents

JOHN RENBOURN'S COMPLETE ANTHOLOGY OF MEDIEVAL & RENAISSANCE MUSIC FOR GUITAR

MW00666803

FREE

Free audio available online!

Visit: www.melbay.com/95394

CD CONTENTS

1 Medley: Lamento Di Tristan & Rotta [2:56]
2 Medley: Trotto/Saltarello [2:33]
3 The English Dance [2:48]
4 Saltarello (Circle Dance) [4:22]
5 Medley: Gypsy Dance & Jew's Dance [3:25]
6 Medley: Bransle Gay & Bransle De Bourgogne [2:48]
7 Bourée I and II [2:19]
8 The Earle Of Salisbury [1:20]
9 The Moon Shines Bright [3:52]
10 Medley: Toye For Two Lutes & My Lord Willoughby's Welcome Home [6:50]
11 Westron Wynde [1:22]
12 Alman [1:52]
13 Medley: Veri Floris & Triple Ballade [2:42]

Visit us on the Web at www.melbay.com — E-mail us at email@melbay.com

For the Flynns

THE MUSIC

Introduction

The title of this collection — *Mel Bay's Complete Anthology of Medieval and Renaissance Music for the Guitar* — may be somewhat misleading. The guitar as we know it, with six single strings, did not emerge until the end of the eighteenth century, so, strictly speaking I suppose, there really isn't any music specifically for the instrument before that time. Also, of course, the body of early music is vast and this volume contains only a small number of selected pieces. However, for some time now I have periodically made transcriptions of early pieces mainly for my own enjoyment and, since virtually all of these are contained here, in effect this book represents the "complete collection" of my medieval and Renaissance arrangements.

My own interest in early music runs parallel to my interest in western folk music. It was, and still is, intriguing to consider the characteristics that are common in both — the same old modal framework and the recurrence of particular note groupings, as well as strong metric and rhythmic similarities. I discovered that even whole pieces, thought to exist only in manuscript, occasionally cropped up remarkably intact in current folk playing, and instruments long assumed silent were found to be still sounding in remote areas of Europe. At some point I began trying out the application of one approach to the other, by taking a medieval dance tune and treating it as I would a jig or reel, or drawing on contrapuntal practice in making arrangements of folk songs.

After a while I found myself with arrangements of a variety of pieces from the Middle Ages and the Renaissance. These were ones that appealed to me for their inherent musical characteristics, not simply because they were old and venerable. Quite often the attraction lay in the use of scale or mode — the arresting rise to the minor seventh at the opening of "Lamento di Tristan" for example, or the freshness of the major mode in "Stantipes" and "English Dance," that must at the time have had a heady effect. Or again, in contrast to these, the almost bizarre melodic content of "Der Judentanz." Others I liked largely for their phrasing and rhythmic makeup — the sneaky additive measures of the second "Saltarello" which contributes so much to the construction of the piece, and the underlying patterns of "Trotto," asymmetrical yet still eminently danceable. Then there were the developing concepts of early part-writing, the great period of Guillaume de Machaut, whose three-part canonic ballade maintains a spacious sense of modality while employing almost an entire chromatic scale, and later the schools of Renaissance counterpoint with works by Byrd and Dowland, both of whom made settings of popular tunes that have endured in the folk tradition. Pieces of this type are all included here, not as dry examples of period style but because each one has its own particular magic.

As to the original instrumentation of the pieces, the earlier dance tunes would probably have been played on whatever came to hand; blown, plucked or bowed. A number of the arrangements, though, are specifically for plucked instruments, such as the gittern, vihuela, bandora and lute. Others are keyboard pieces and even reductions of consort settings. I like to play them on the steel-string guitar. Metal-strung instruments have a long pedigree, going back to the medieval harp, and include the bandora, orpharion and cittern. I find that the balance and sustain of steel strings can be effective both for the dance tunes and for the more intricate contrapuntal pieces. This is not meant to deter the classical guitarist, who is probably already aware of at least some of the pieces, but rather to put forward the steel-string as being well-suited to music of this type. The nylon-strung guitar has already inherited a good deal from the lute and vihuela repertoire but nearly all of the other arrangements here should work equally well.

What may appear unusual, though, are some of the tunings used in the arrangements. Steel-string players are largely familiar with a range of altered tunings — tunings that were in common use in the nineteenth century parlor repertoire and continued on in the American folk styles, tunings that have evolved since then in imitation of the mountain banjo, and others that came into being through the arrangement of modal folksong as well as in more contemporary approaches. Classical players, however, sometimes tend to regard altered tunings with suspicion, partly, I suppose, because nylon strings are less amenable to changes of tension, but mainly, I suspect, because they throw the player into unfamiliar territory. Although some of the tunings I have used may seem peculiar at first sight, often they are little more than the principal notes of the mode of the piece, and really are not difficult to come to grips with. The standard tuning that settled in with the introduction of the sixth string offers the most harmonic potential, but is usually less effective for the performance of modal, or pre-tonal, music. I find that altered tunings can really enhance an arrangement, so, rather than to limit the collection to accurate but conventional settings, I have opted for those that come to life even if they appear a little unorthodox.

The main thing, of course, is to enjoy playing the pieces. They do all work. I have lived with them long enough and they still excite me every time I come back to them.

JOHN RENBOURN.

Lamento di Tristan — Rotta

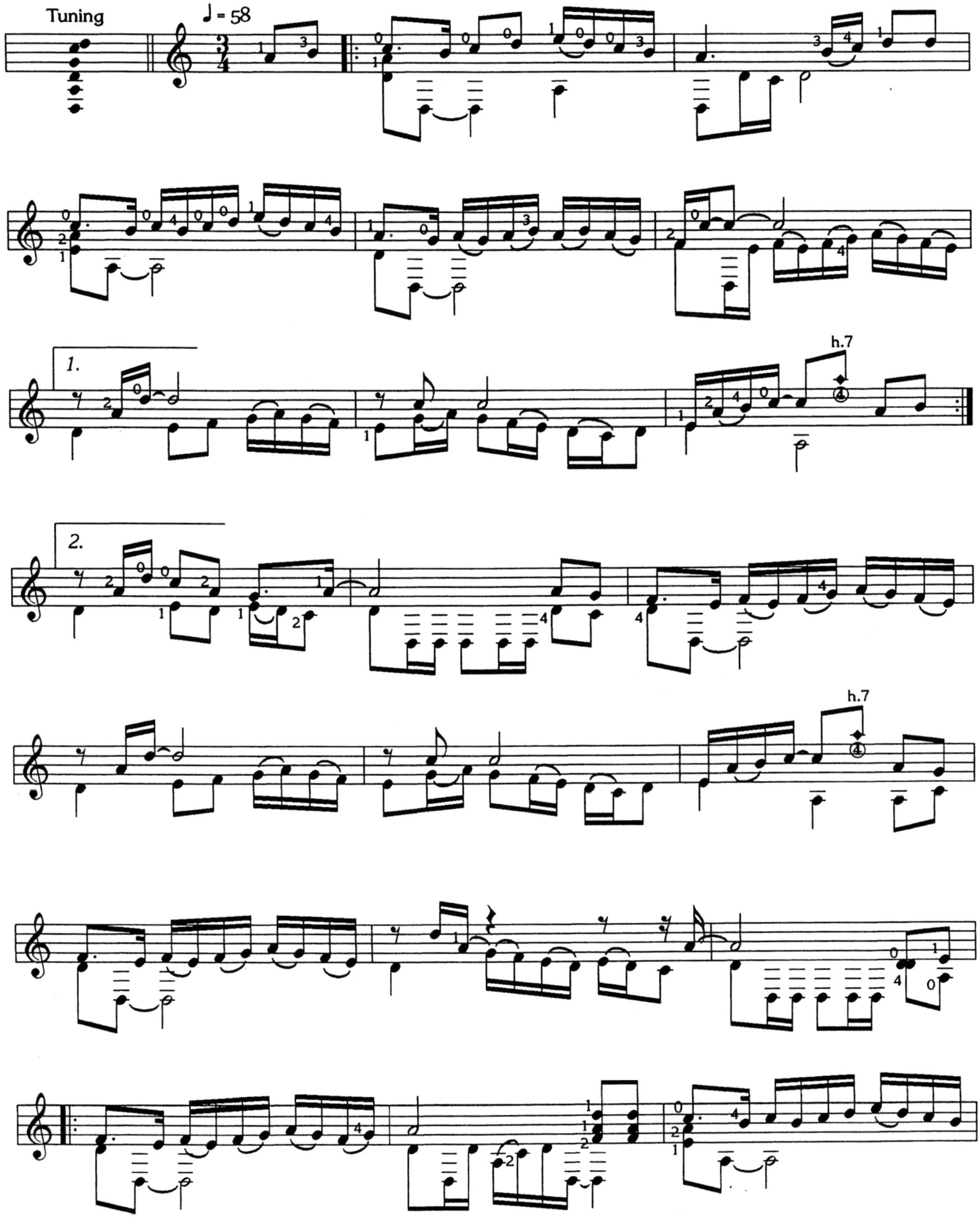

1.
h.7
2
♩ = 96
IX

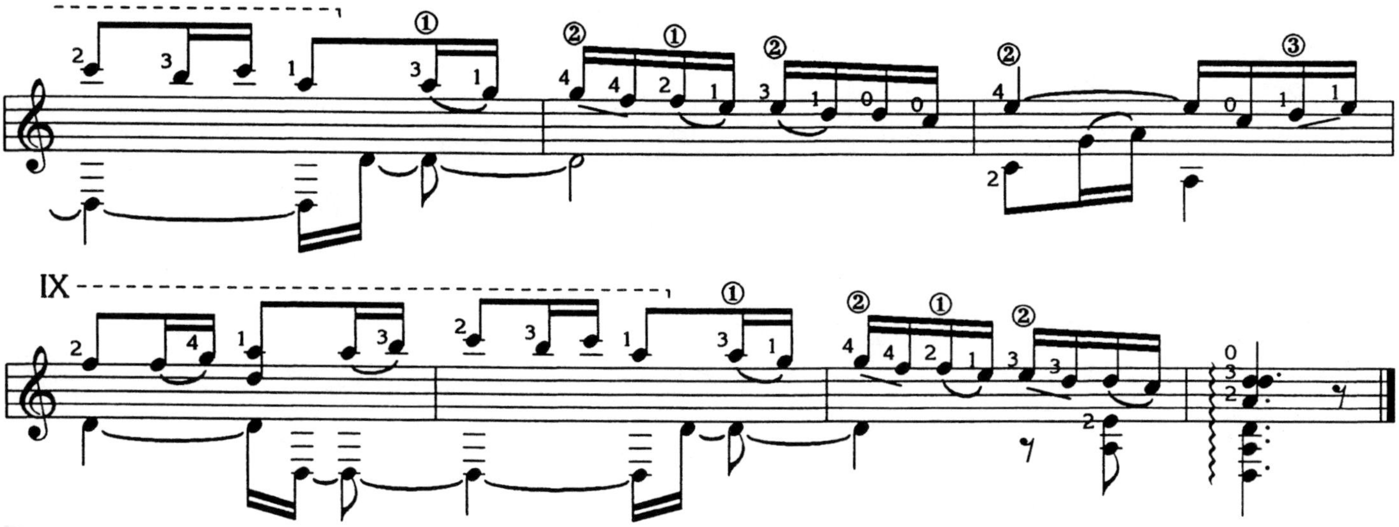

Lamento di Tristan — Rotta

Tablature

2.

1.
2.
♩ = 96
<7>

SALTARELLO

1.
2.
1.
2.

Saltarello
Tablature

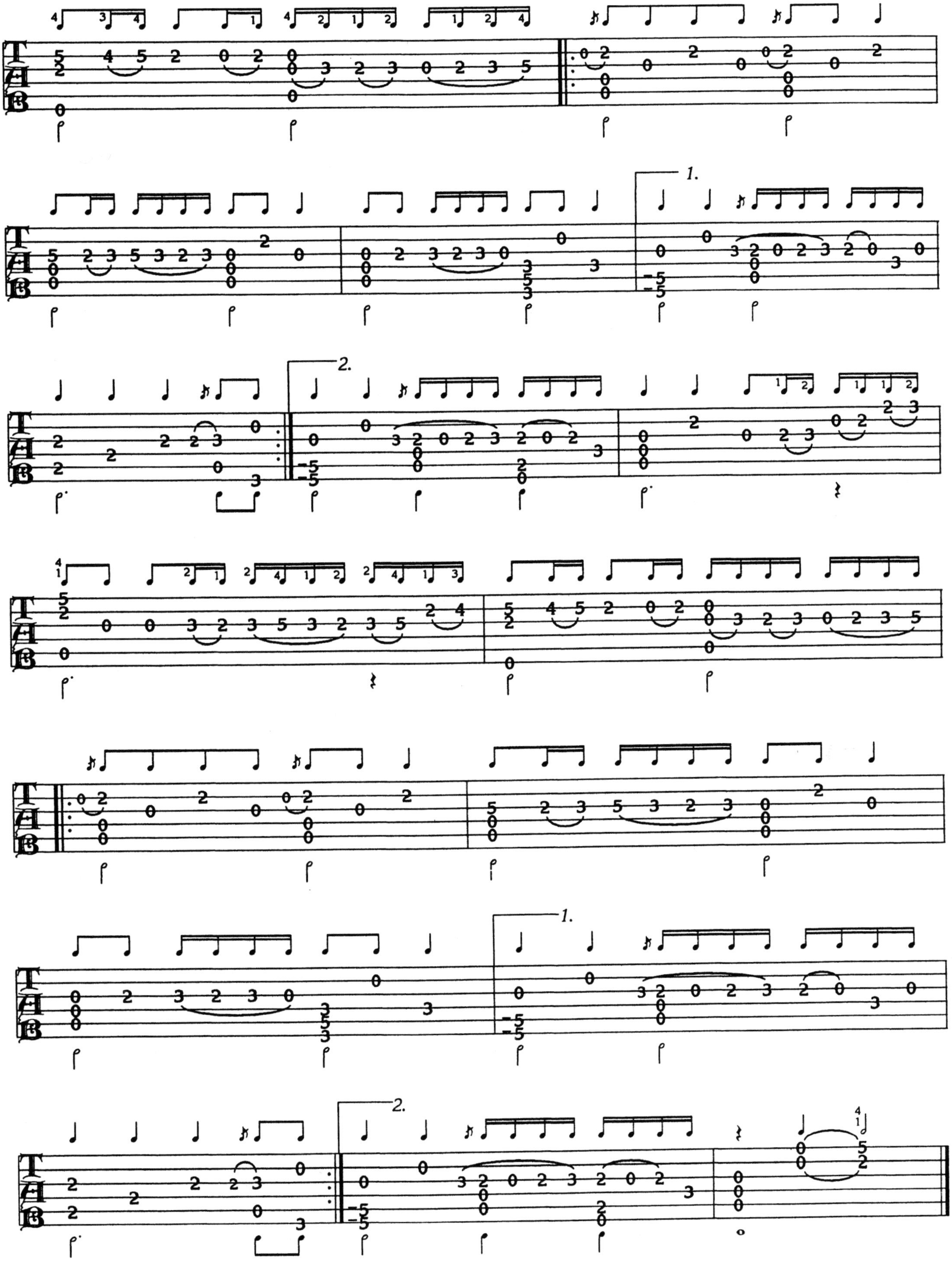

Trotto

Trotto
Tablature

STANTIPES

STANTIPES

Tablature

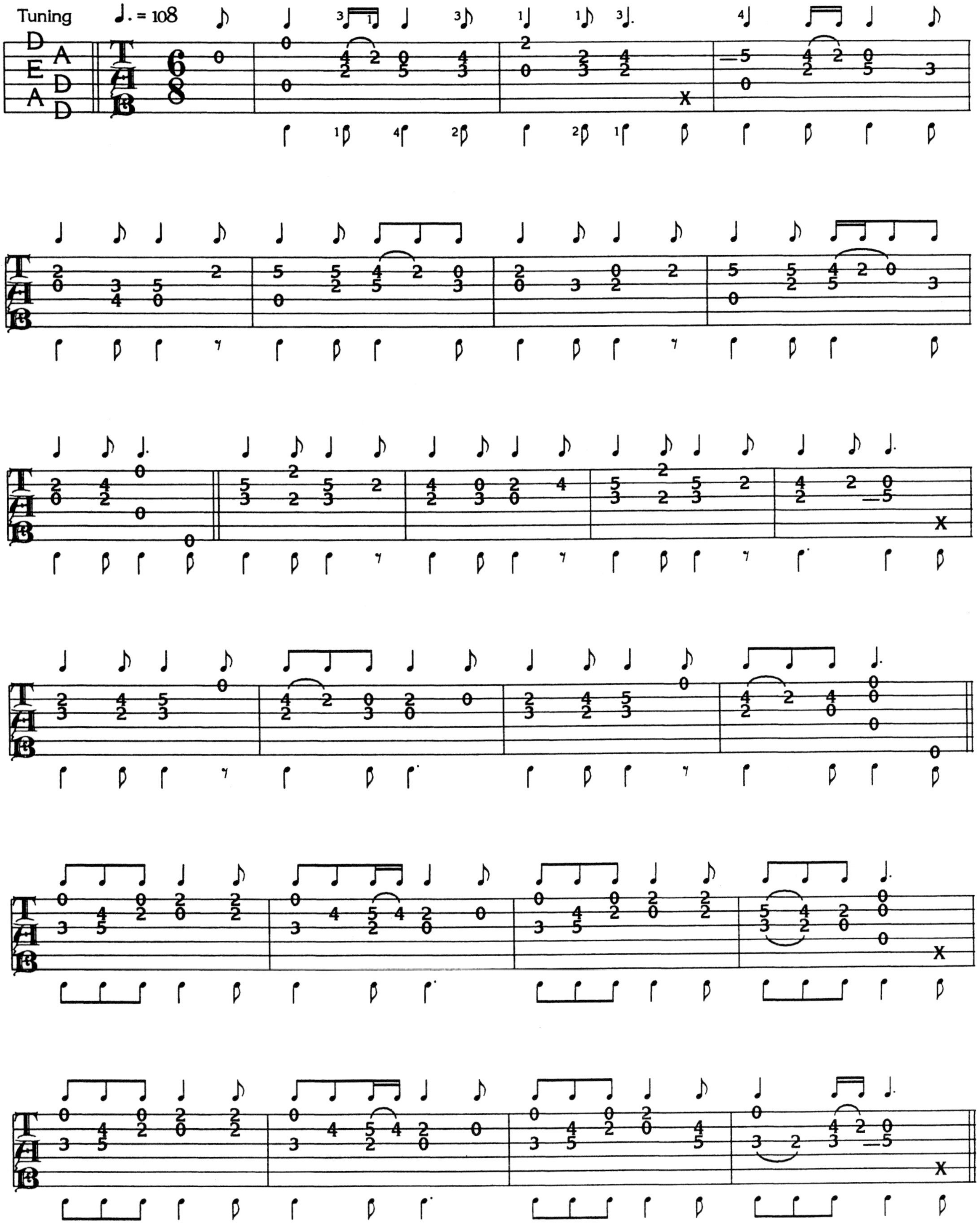

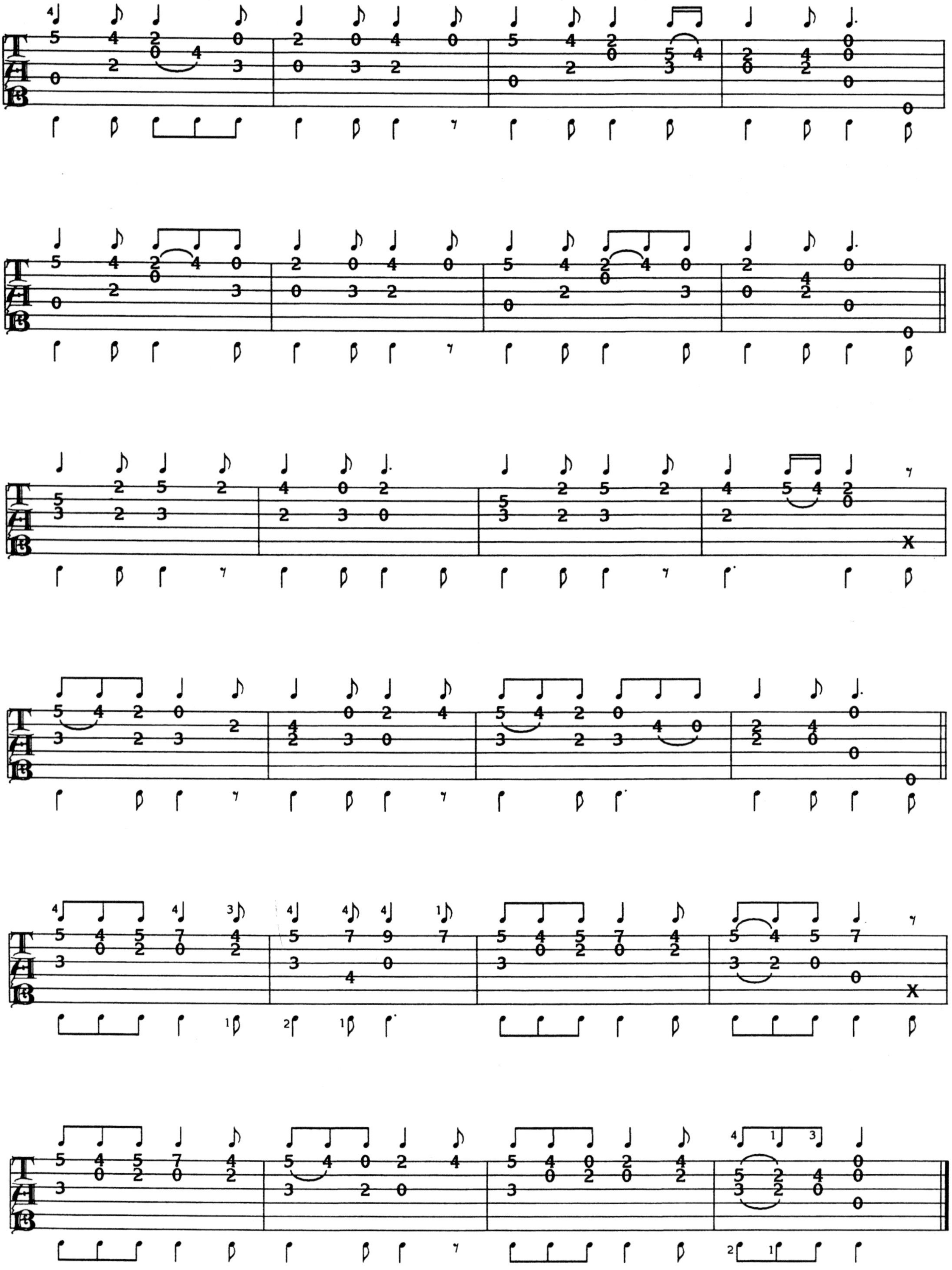

THE ENGLISH DANCE

II
IV
II
II
IV
II
D.C. al
8va h.7
8va h.5

The English Dance

Tablature

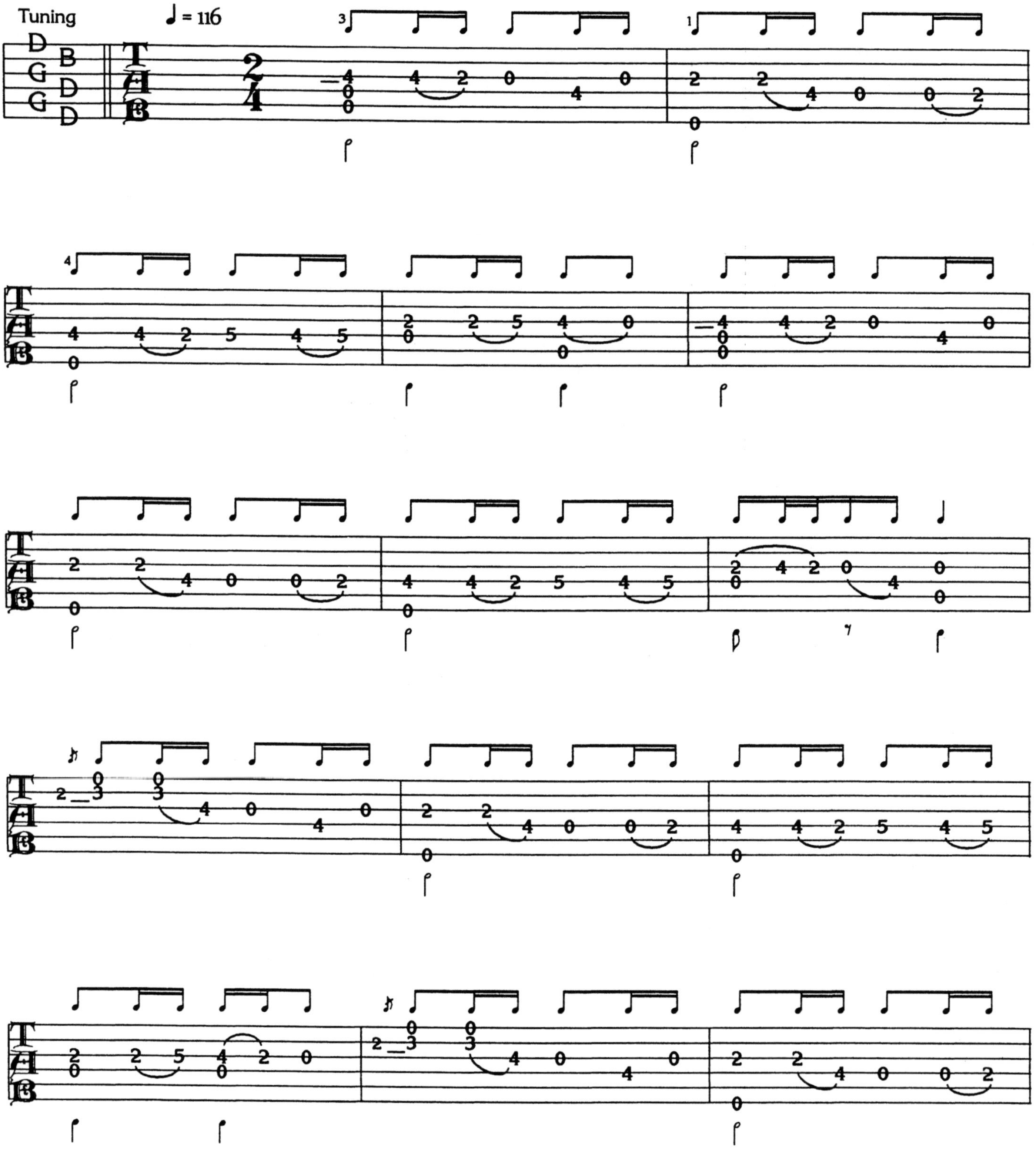

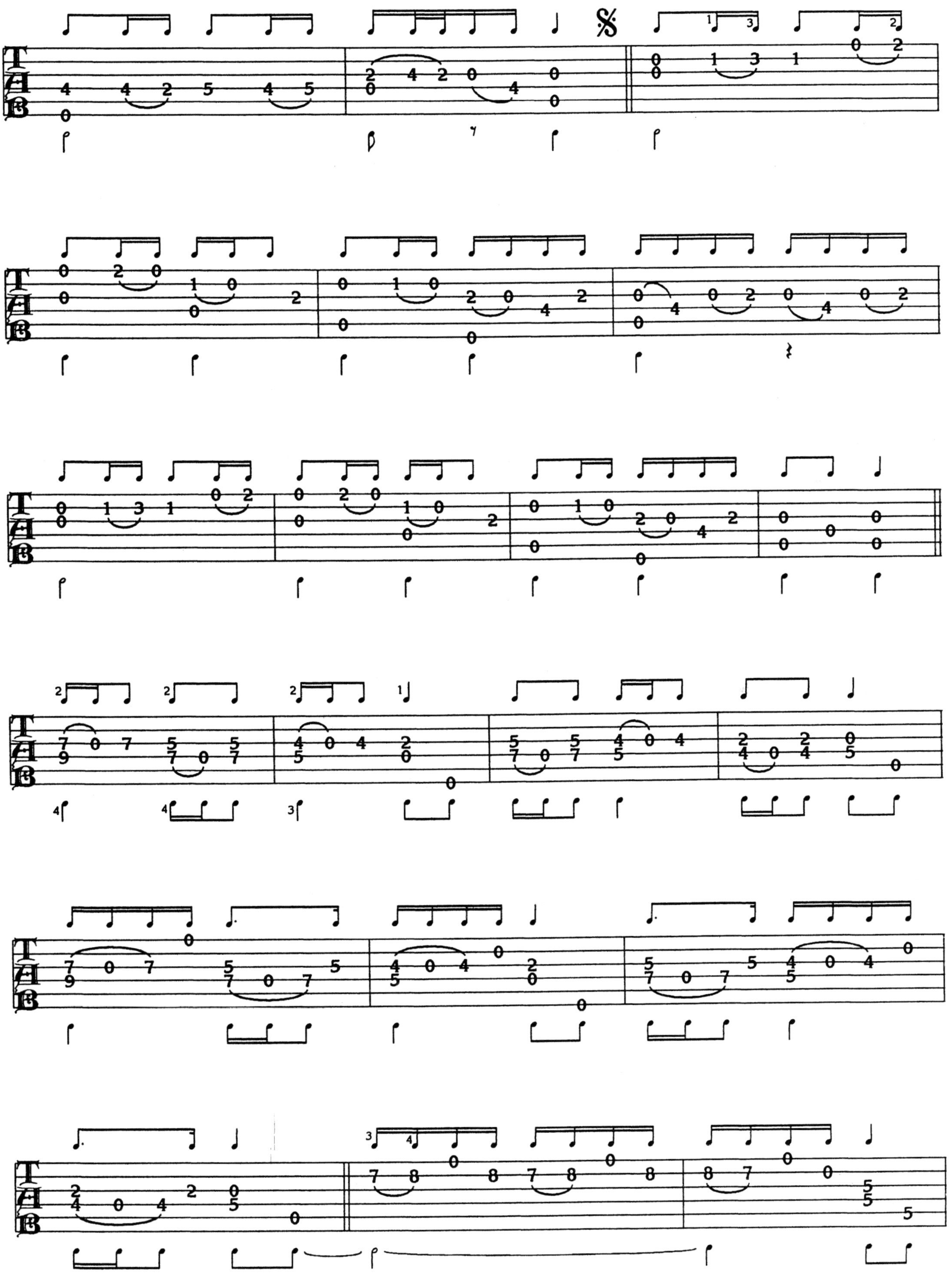

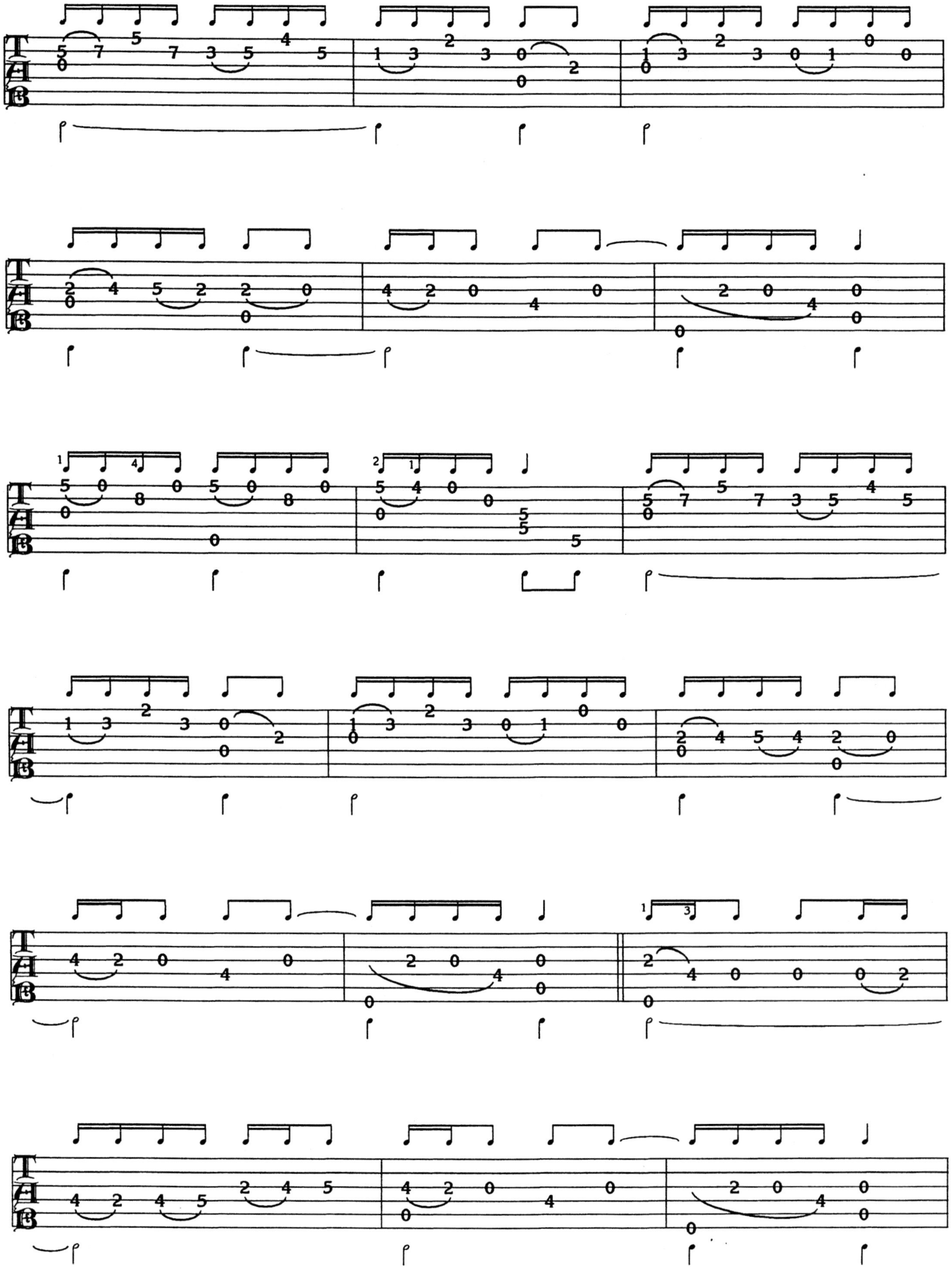

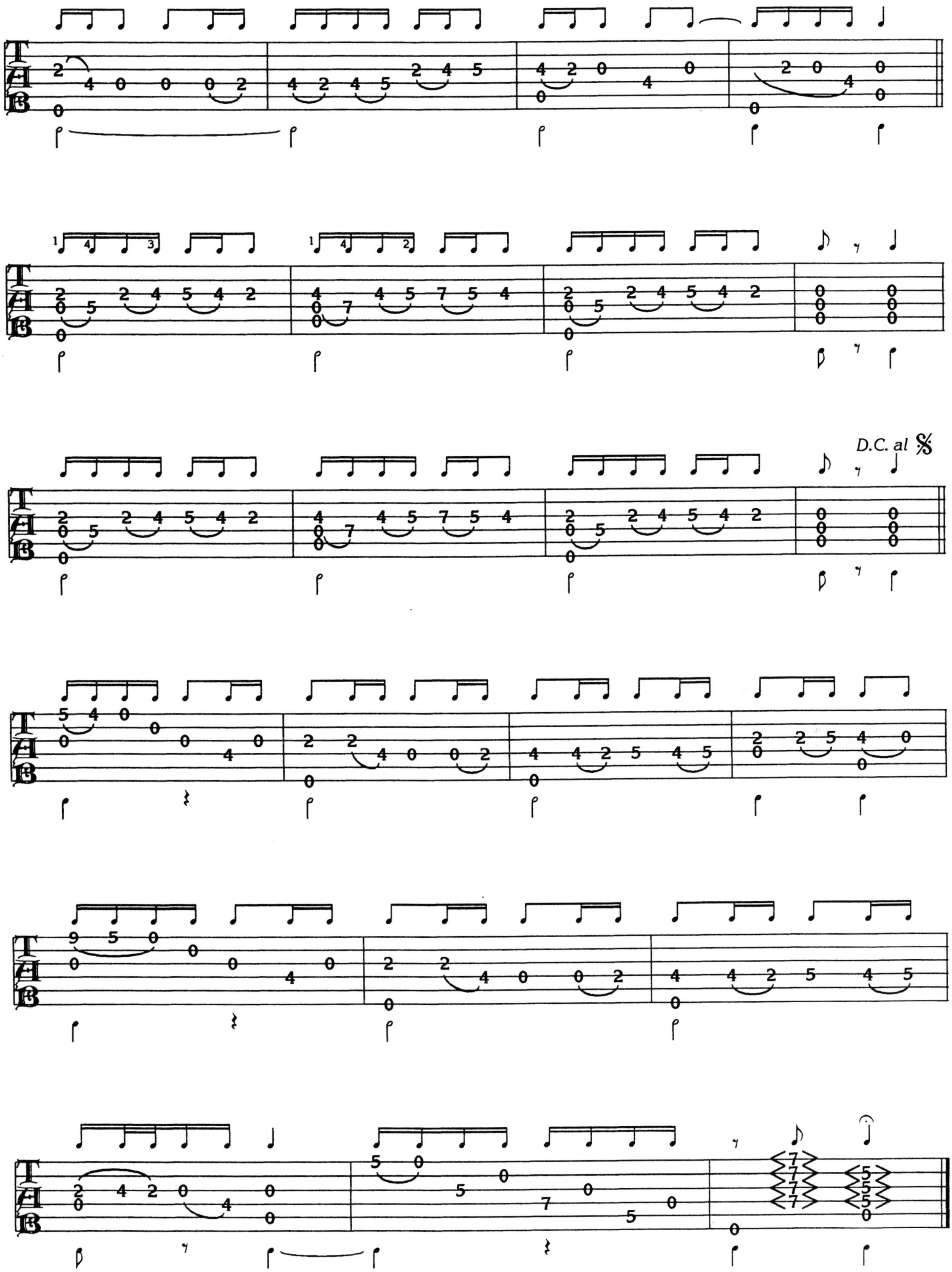
D.C. al

Saltarello

Saltarello

Tablature

Gittern Pavan

GITTERN PAVAN

Tablature

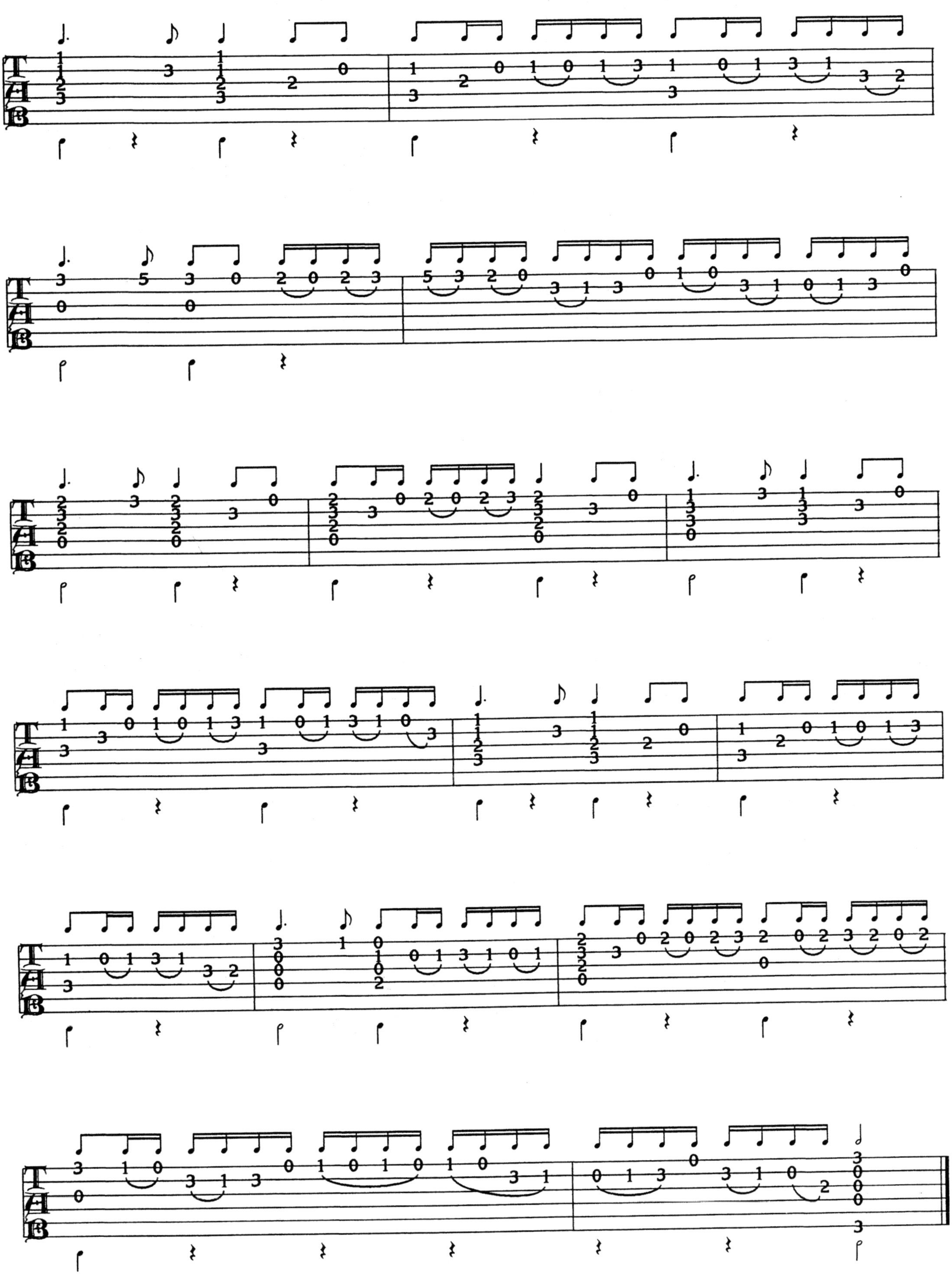

GIPSY DANCE — JEWS' DANCE

Hans Neusiedler

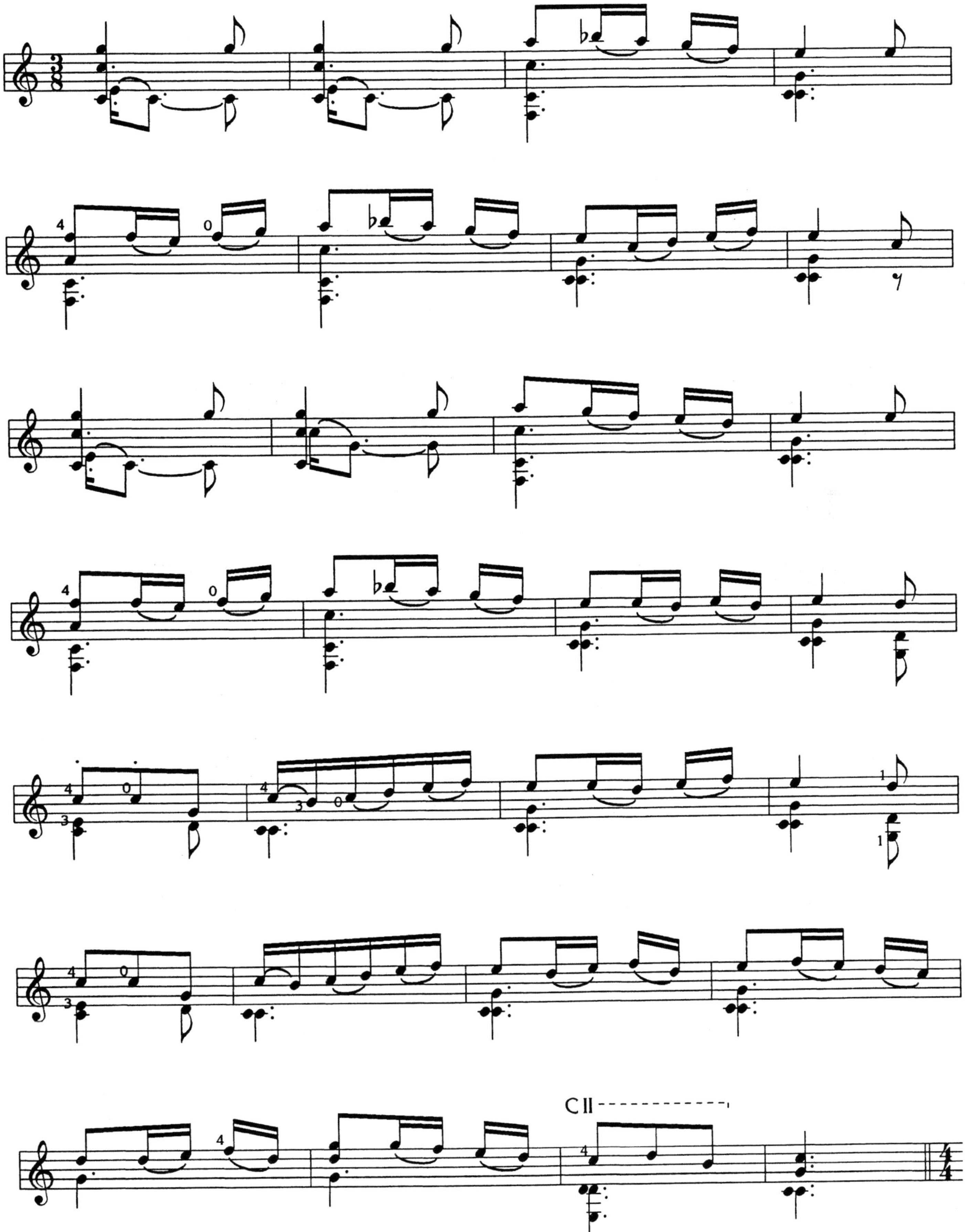
C II

Gipsy Dance — Jews' Dance

Tablature

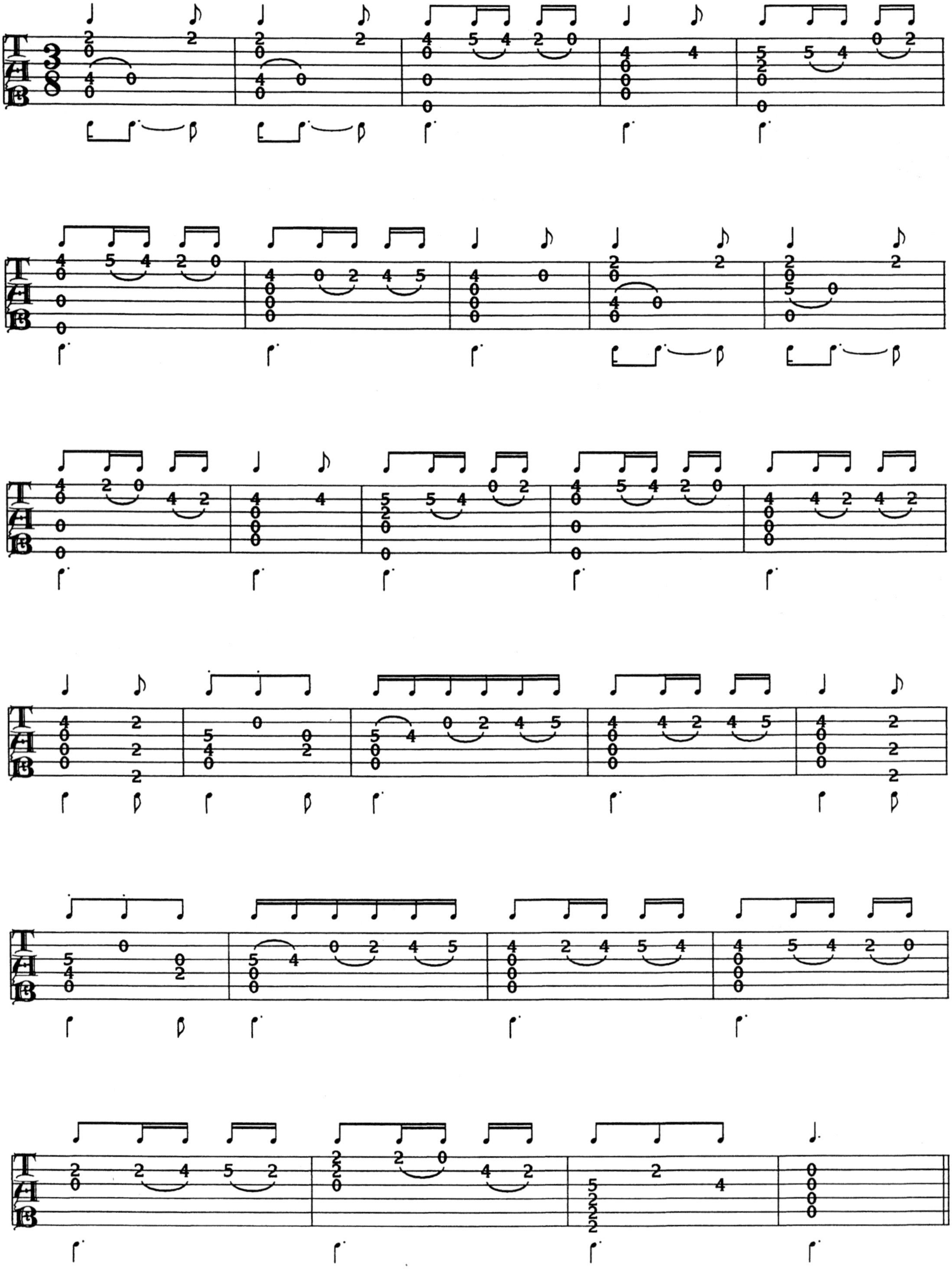

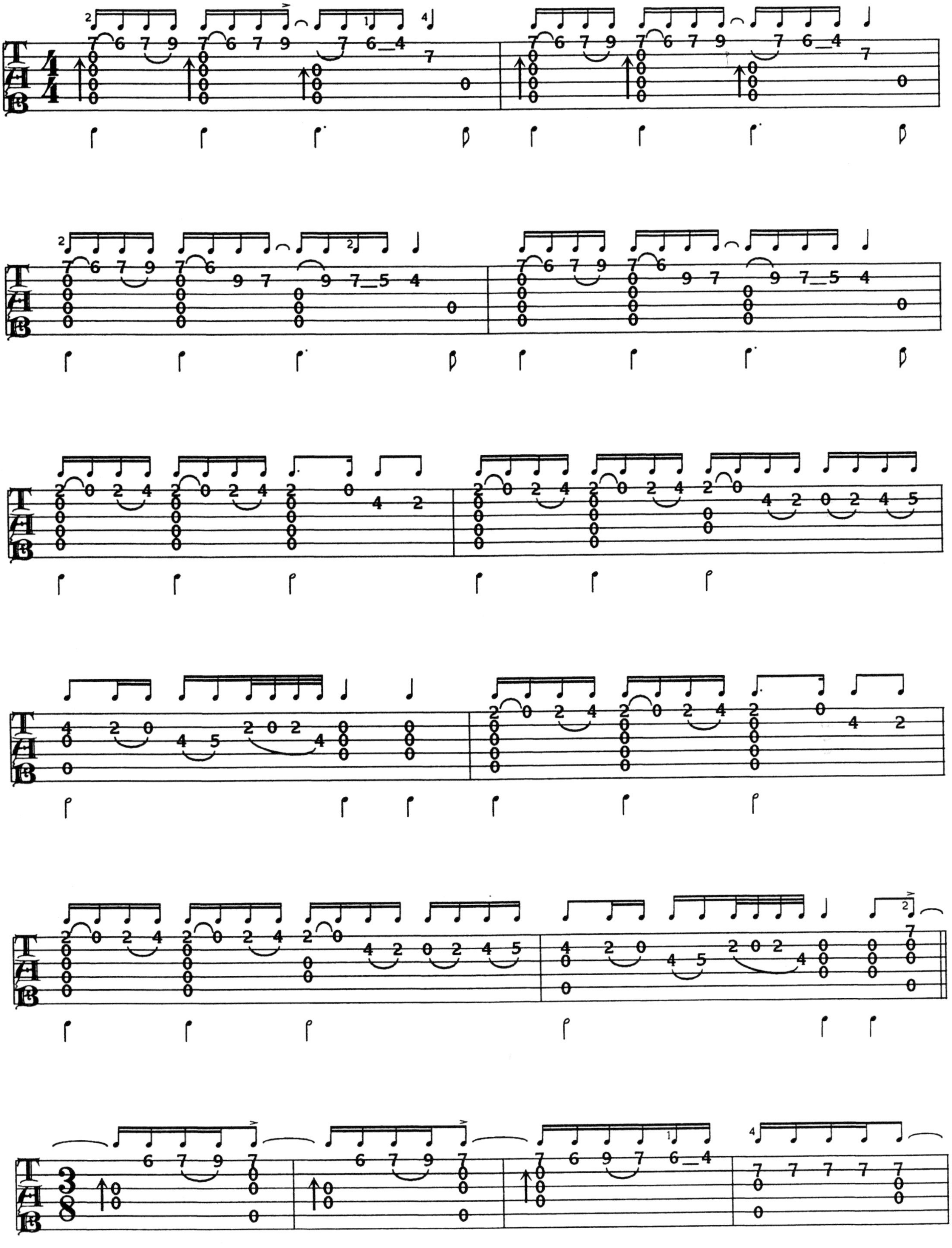

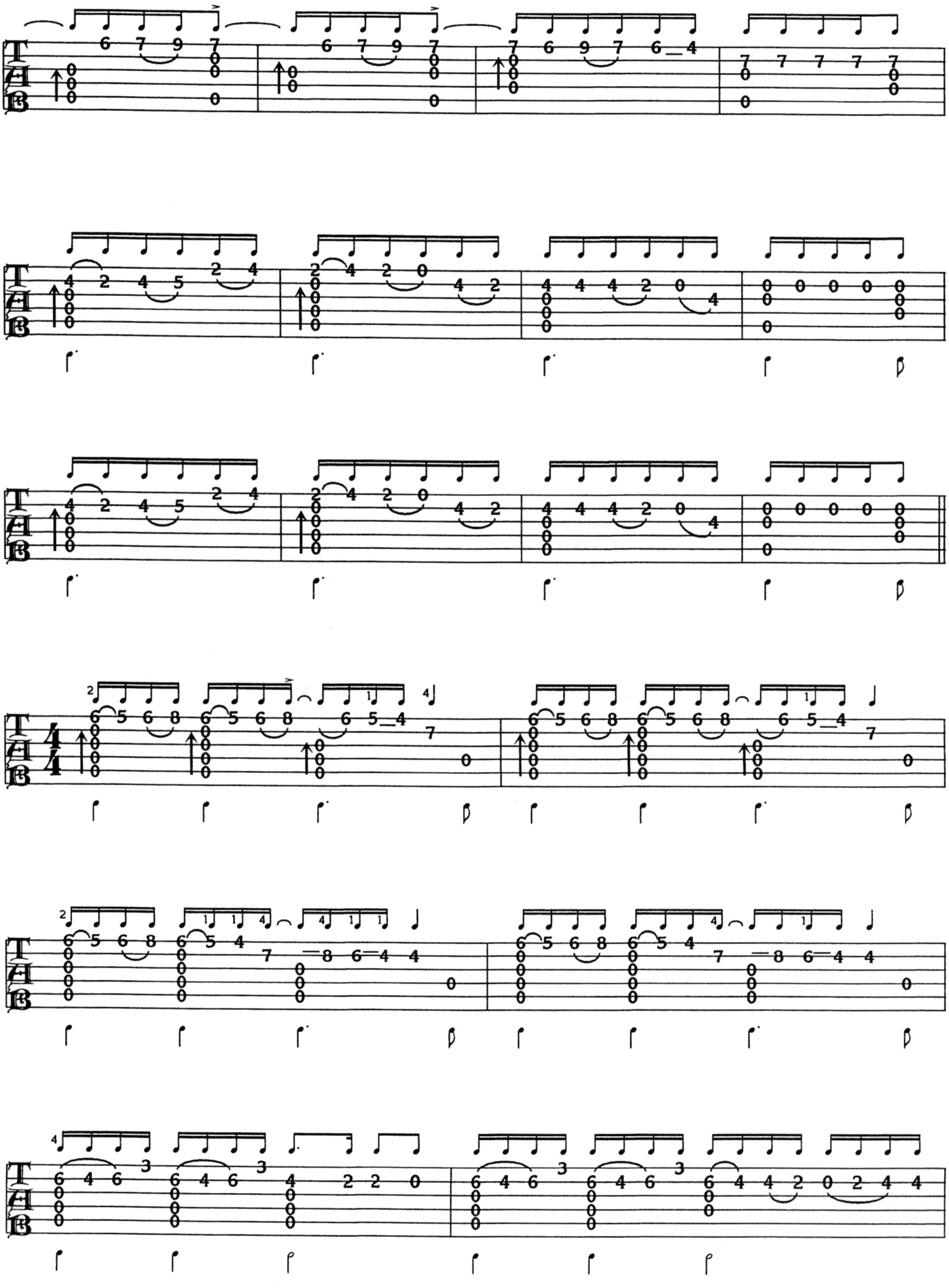

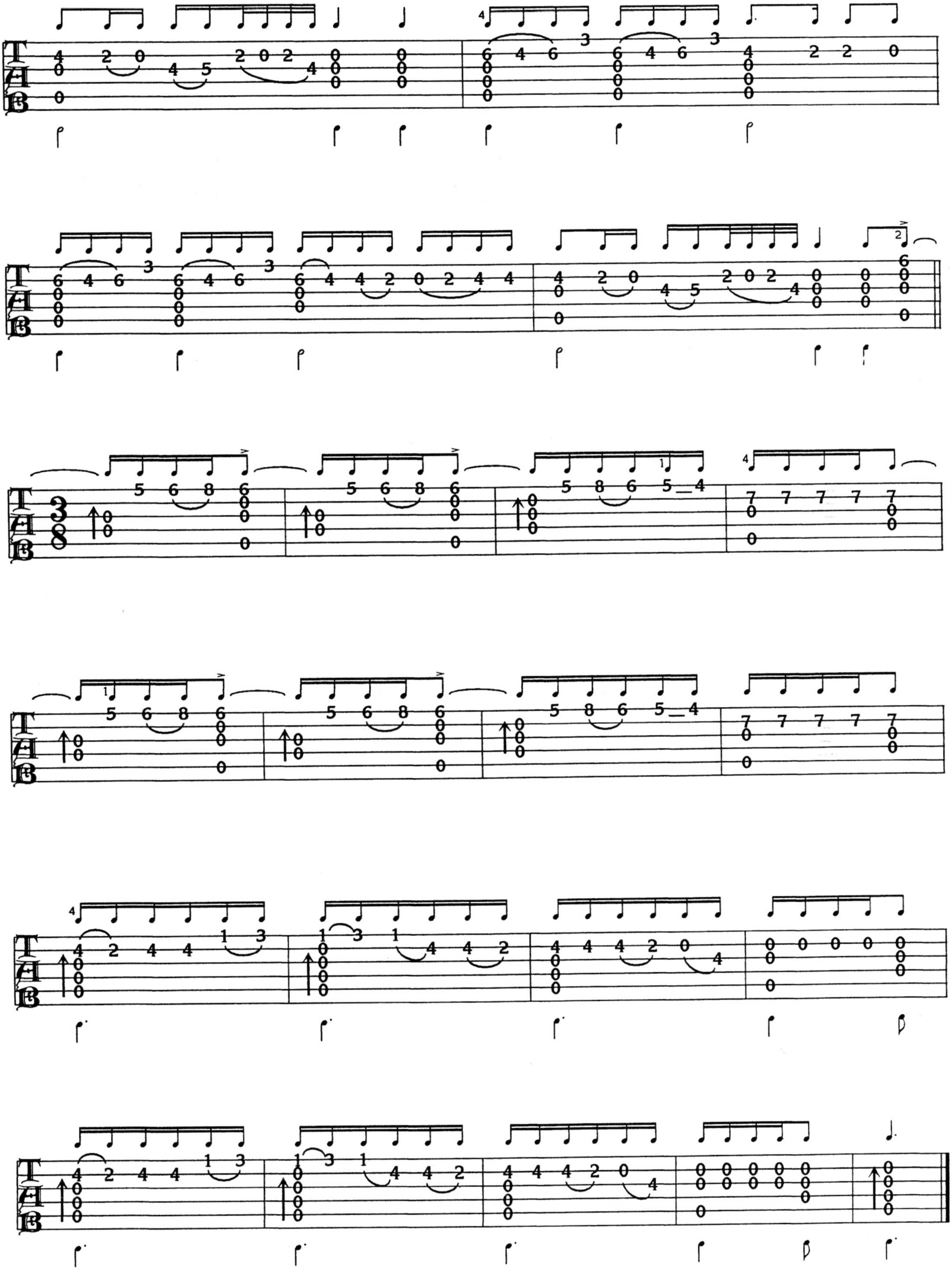

FANTASIA

que contrahaze la harpe en la manera de Luduvico

Alonso Mudarra

C II
C II

C V
C II
C V

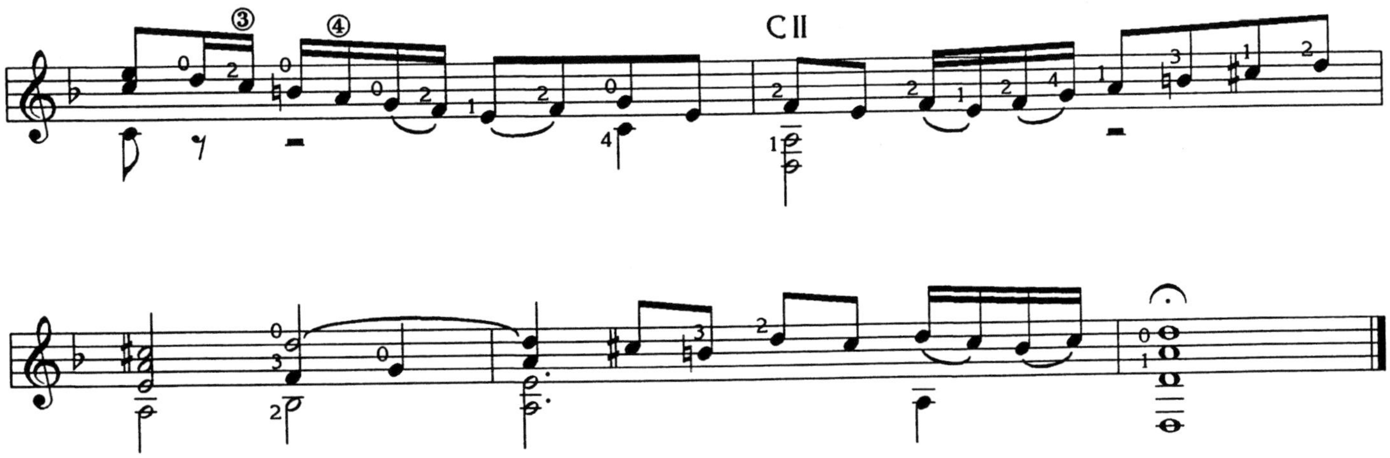

Fantasia

que contrahaze la harpe en la manera de Luduvico

Tablature

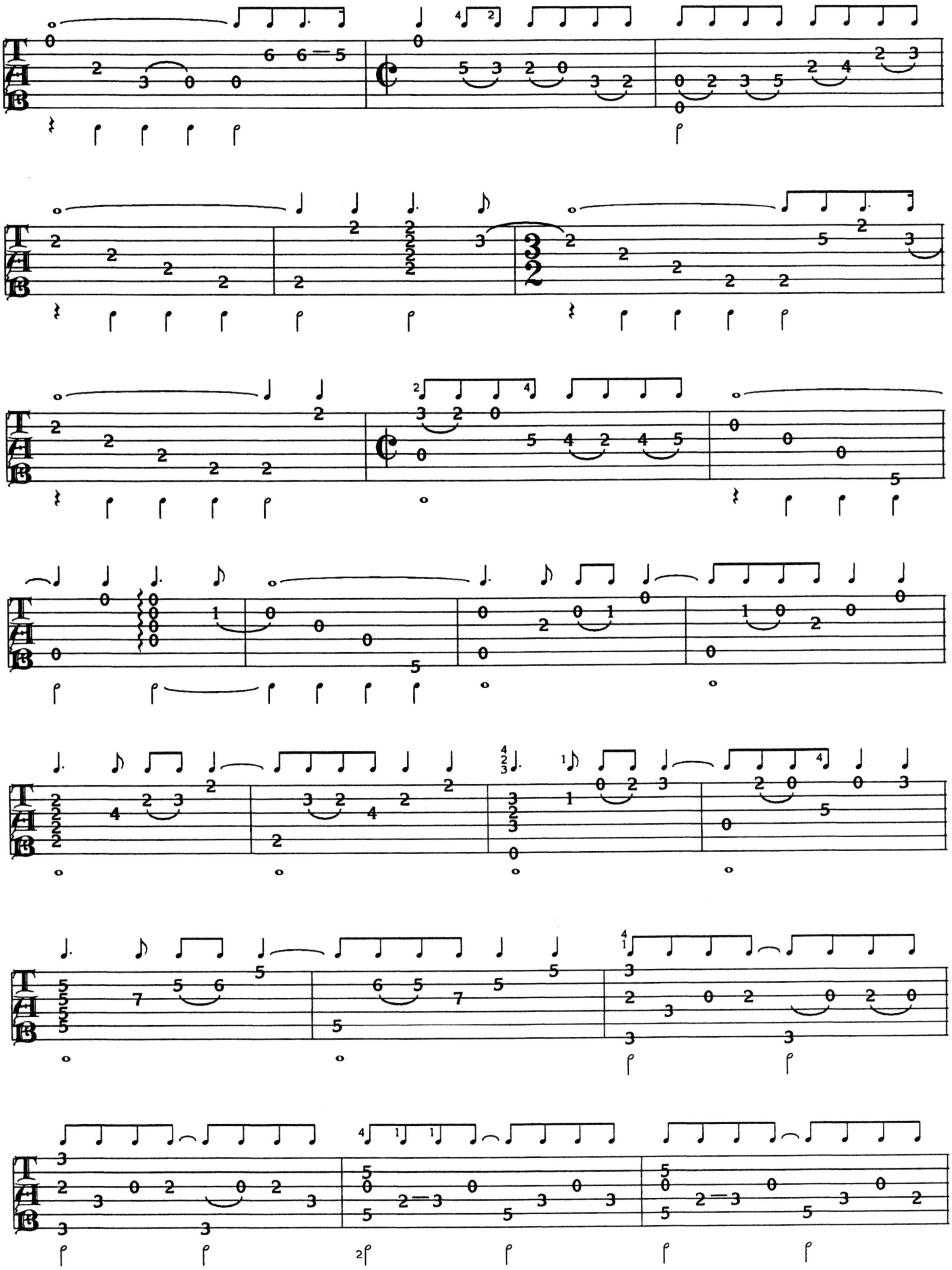

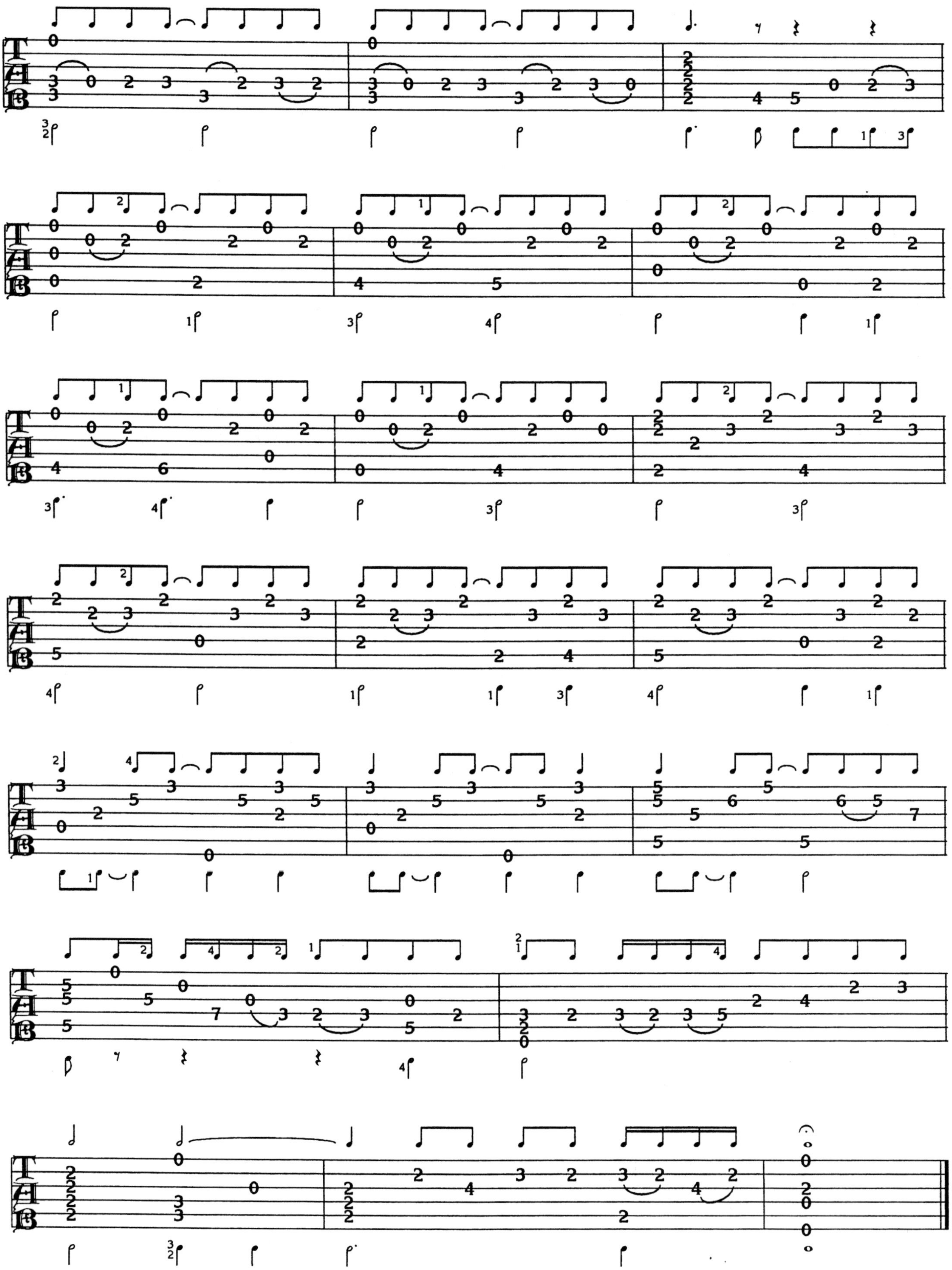

Se Lo M'Accorgo

Se Lo M'Accorgo
Tablature

BRANSLE GAY

Claude Gervaise

Bransle Gay

Tablature

BRANSLE DE BOURGOGNE

Claude Gervaise

BRANSLE DE BOURGOGNE
Tablature

TAB

The Irish Ho-Hoane

The Irish Ho-Hoane

Tablature

Bandora Lullaby

Anthony Holborne

Bandora Lullaby

Tablature

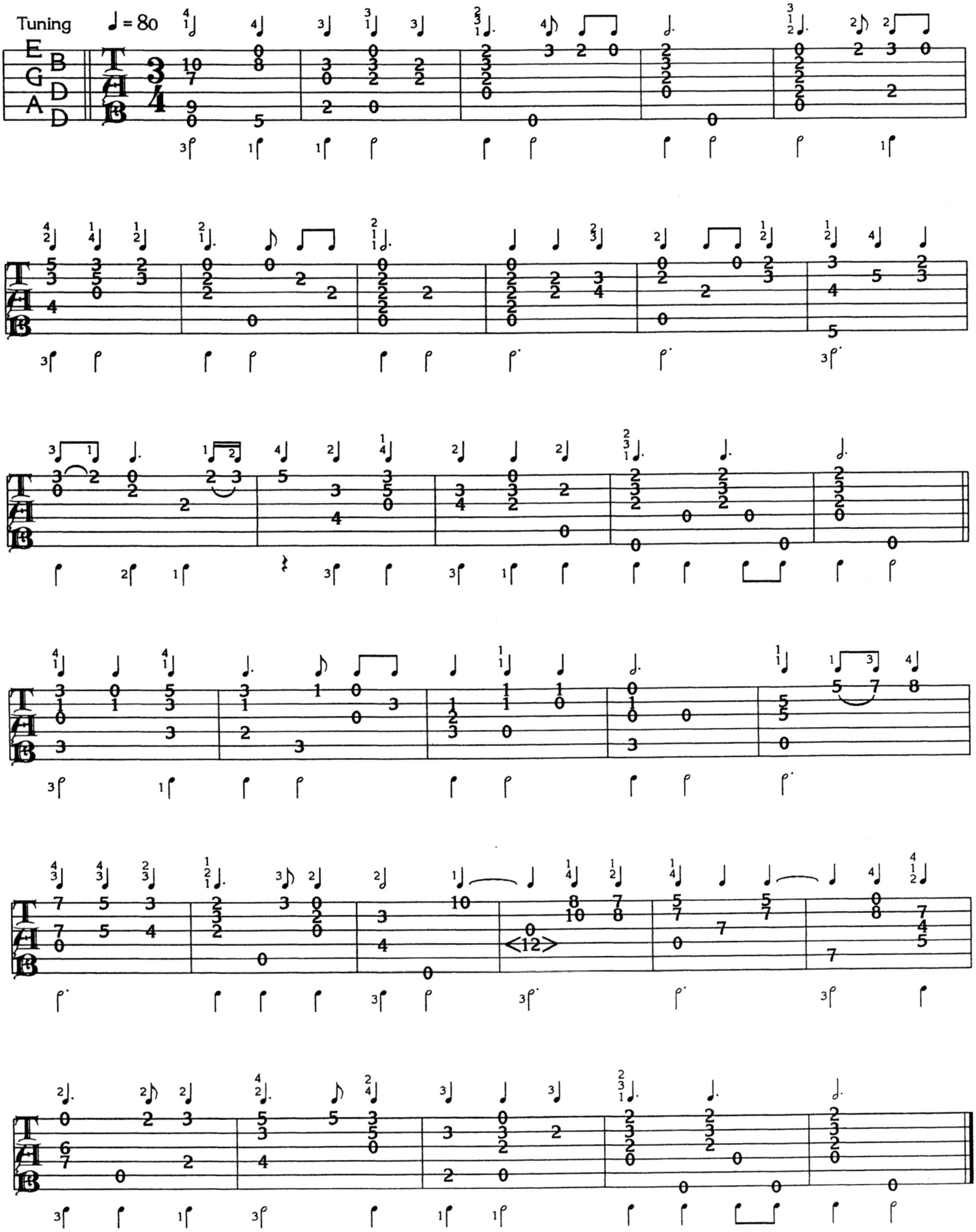

PAVANNE D'ESPAGNE

Nicolas Vallet

Pavanne D'Espagne

Tablature

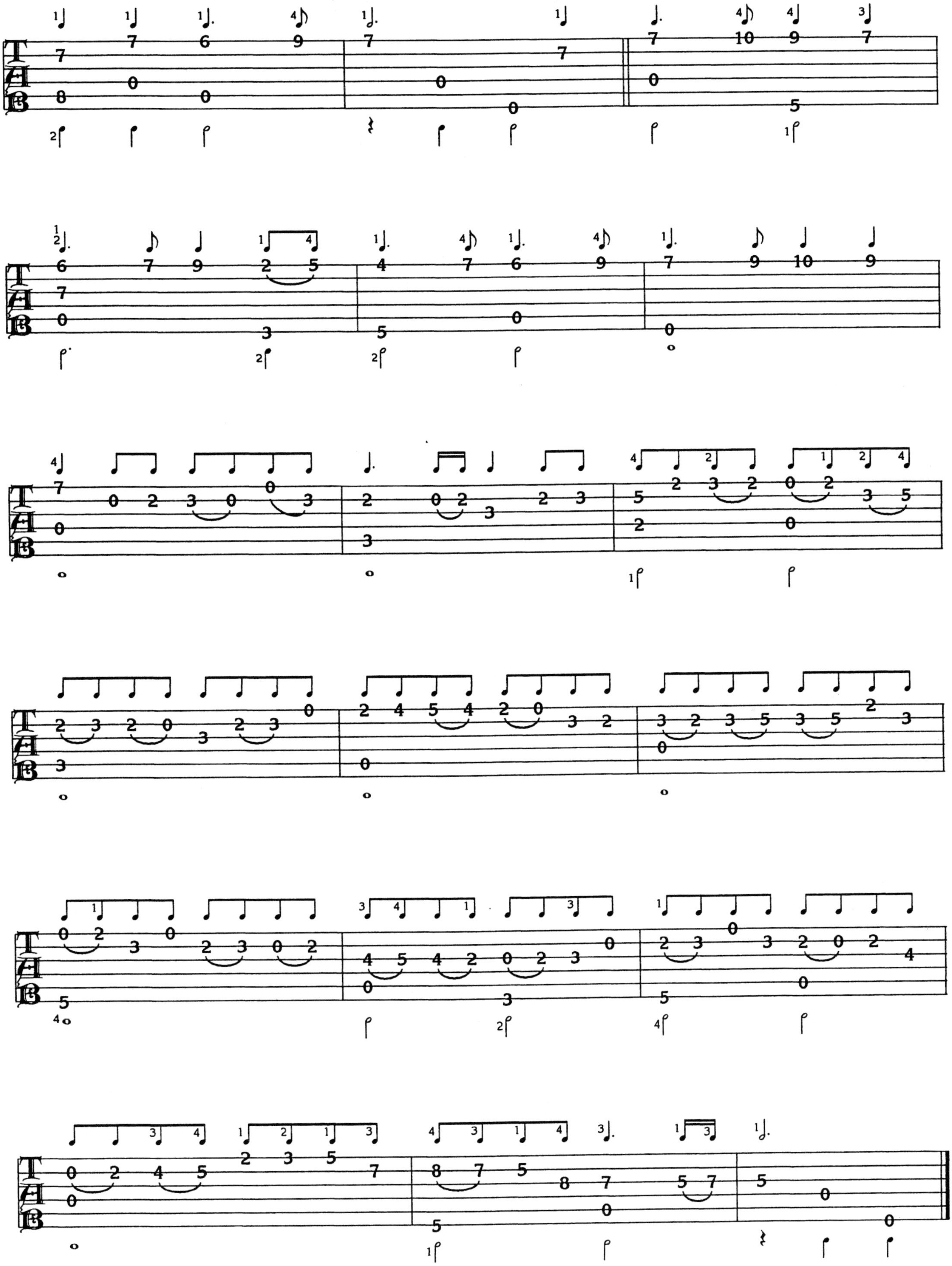

BOURREE I — BOURREE II

Nicolas Vallet

IV
C II

Bourree I — Bourree II

Tablature

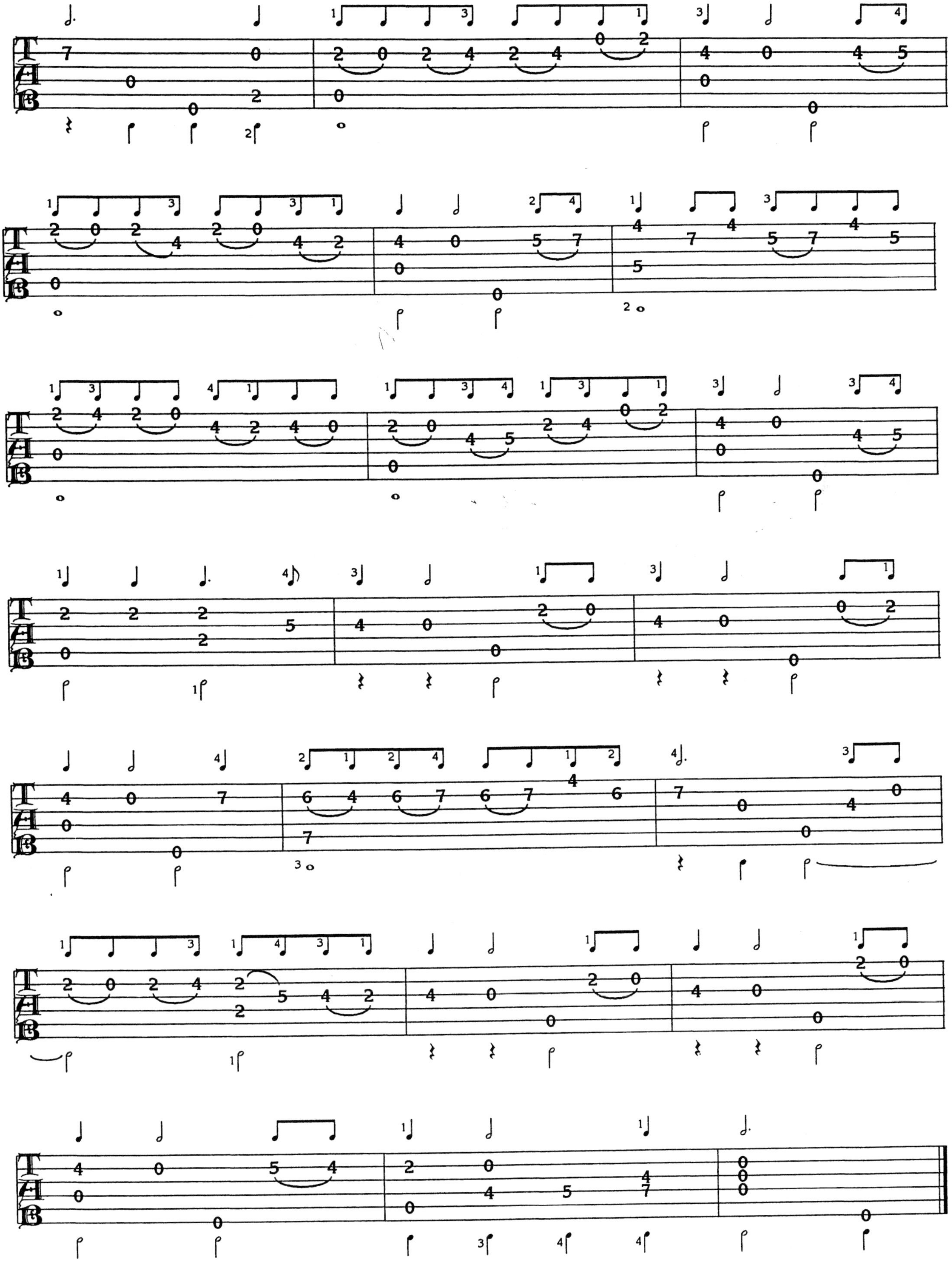

Mal Sims

IV
VII
V
II
IV
II
IV
h.7

Mal Sims
Tablature

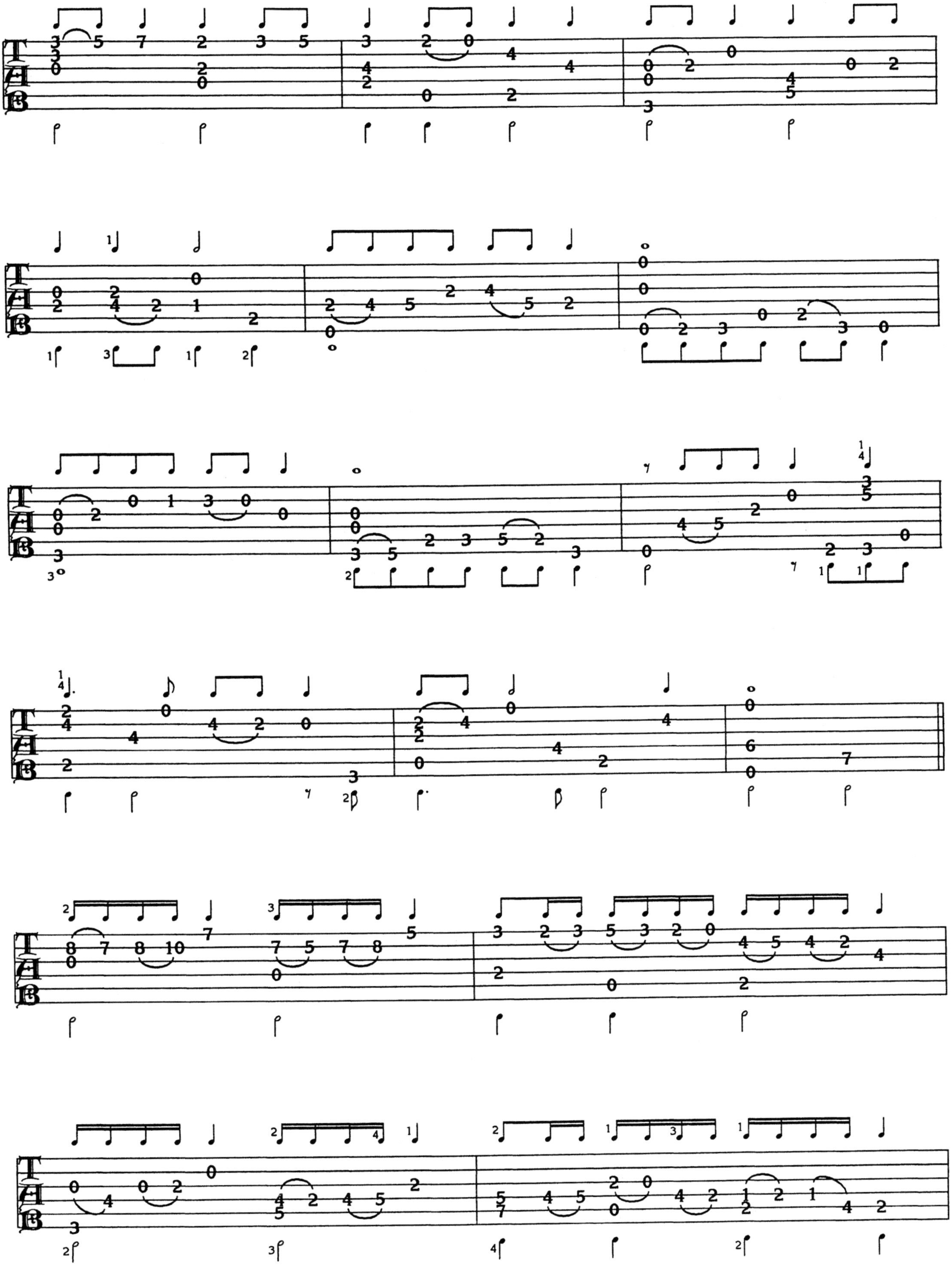

THE EARLE OF SALISBURY

William Byrd

C VII
C V
h.12
h.12
C VII
C V

THE EARLE OF SALISBURY
Tablature

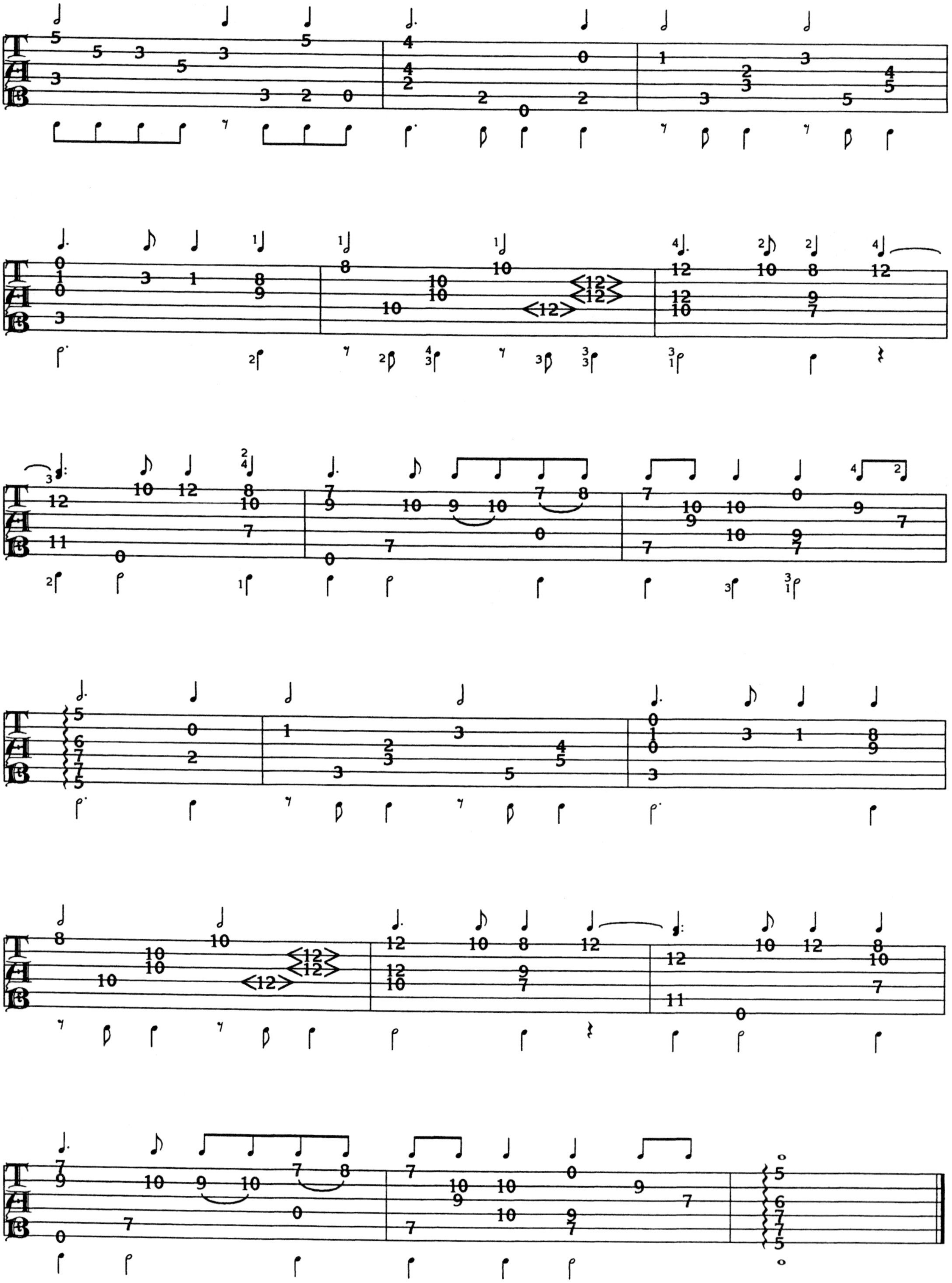

Courante

Robert Ballard

½C II
C II
½C II

COURANTE

Tablature

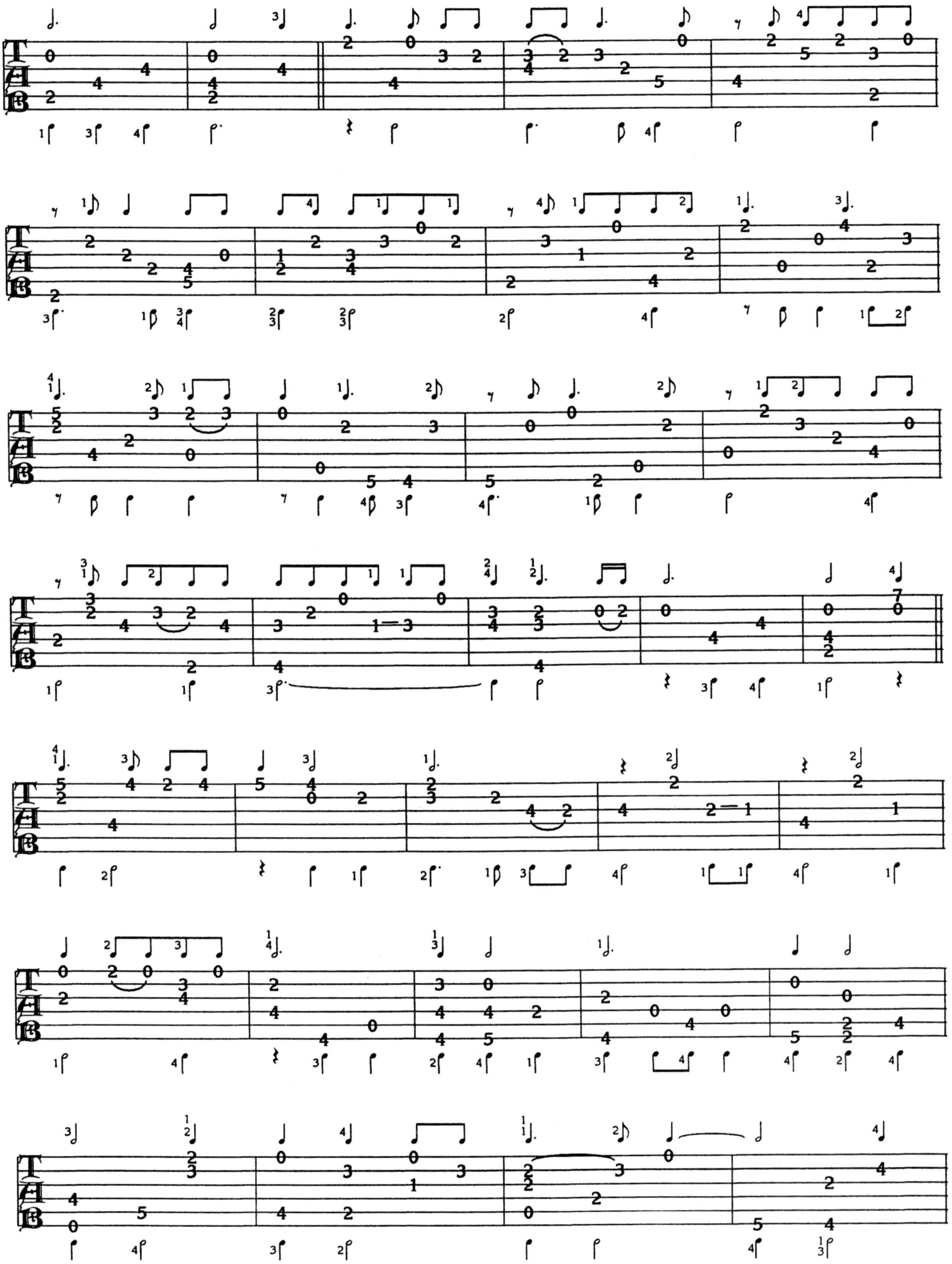

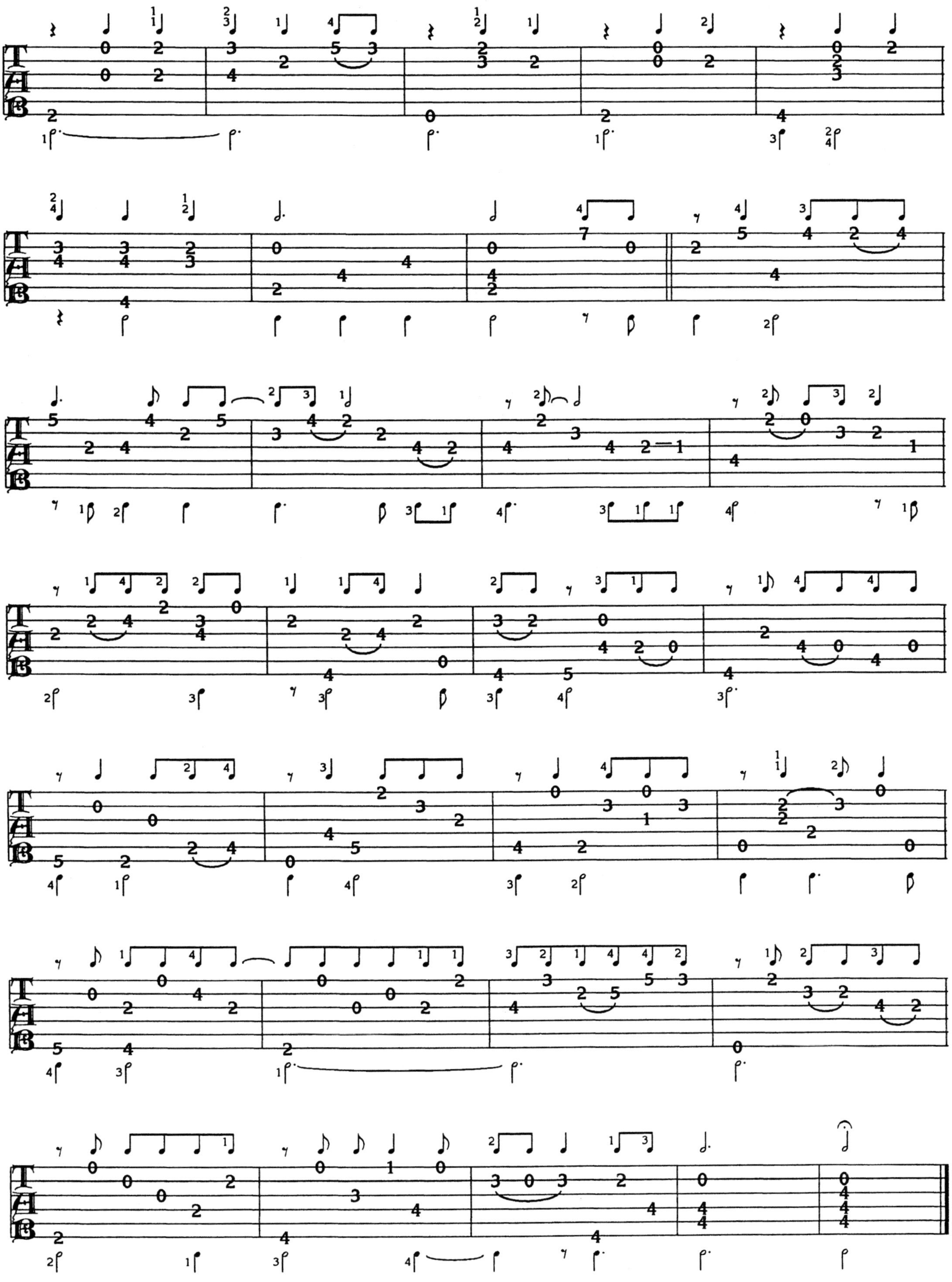

THE MOON SHINES BRIGHT

VII
h.12
h.12
h.7
h.5
V
VII

The Moon Shines Bright

Tablature

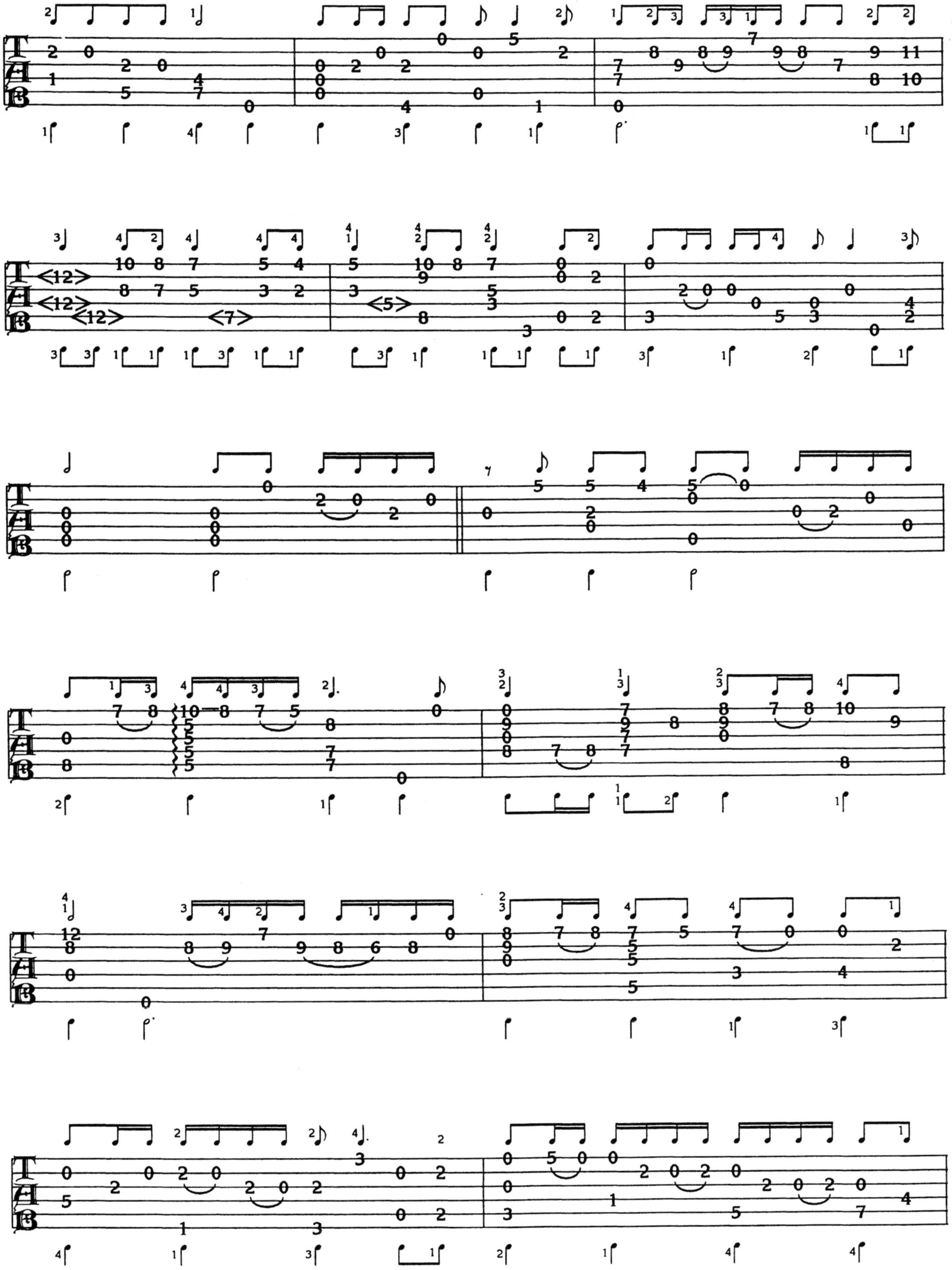

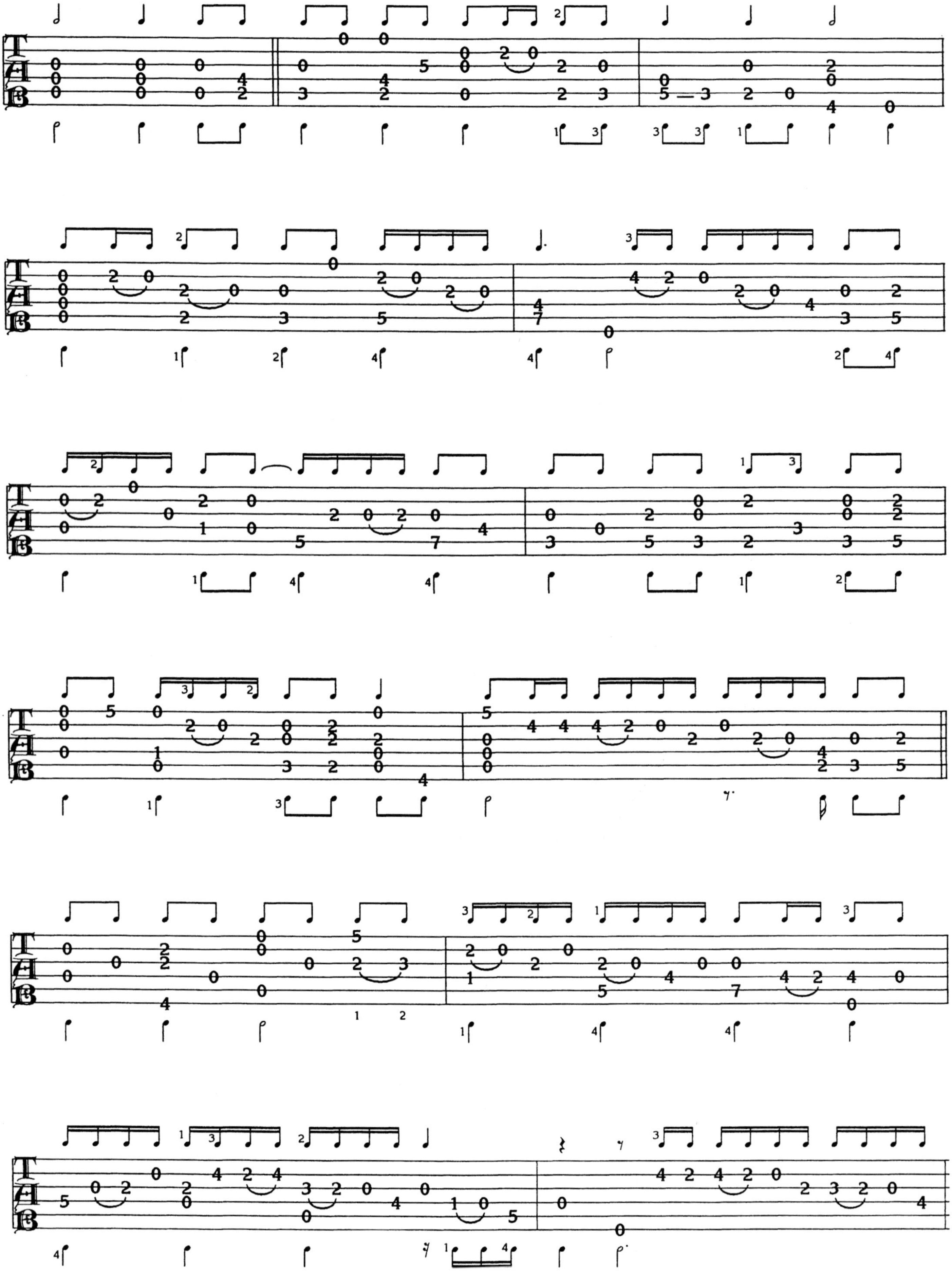

Toy For Two Lutes

Thomas Robinson

Toy For Two Lutes

Tablature

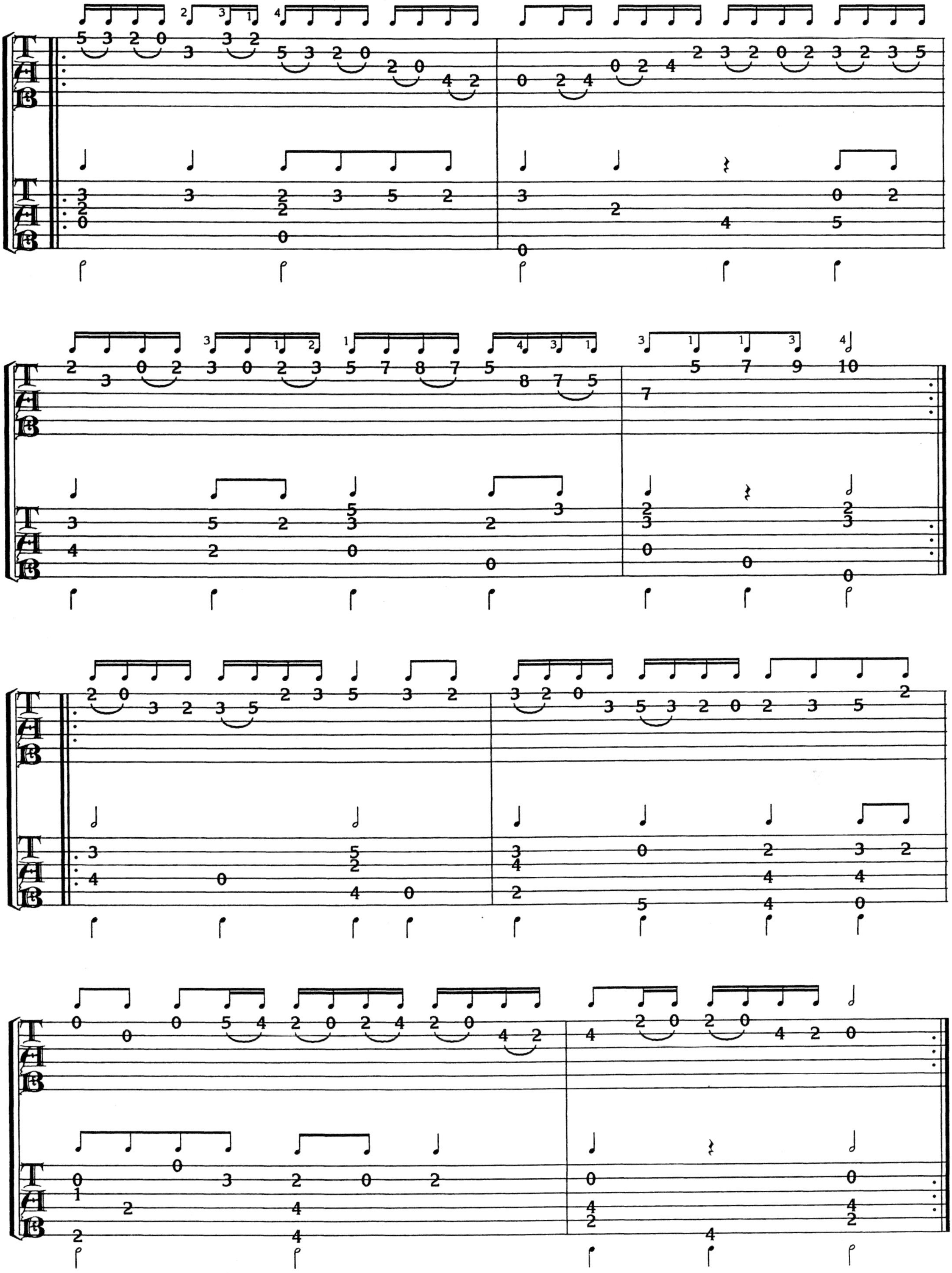

Westron Wynde

The First Section is to be played entirely in Natural Harmonics

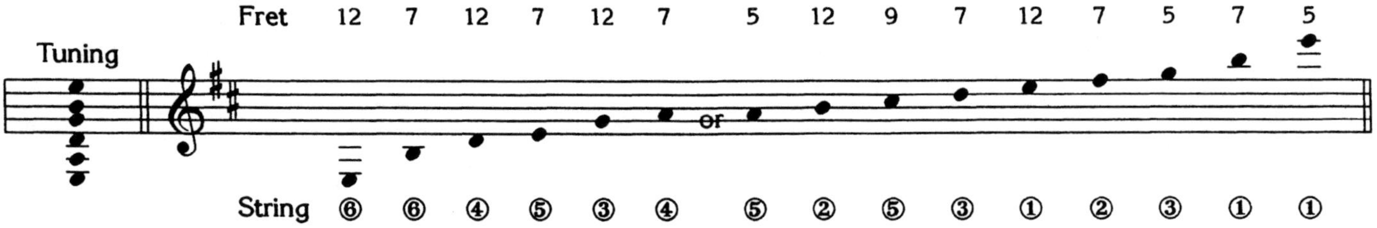

VII
VII
V
VII
V
½C VII
h.12
h.12

V
½C VII
½C V
IV
VII
X
IX
h.12
8va harmonics

Westron Wynde

Tablature

ALMAN

V
II
VII
IV

Alman

Tablature

My Lord Willobie's Welcome Home

h.12
h.12
IX
VII
IX
VII

½C XII
h.12
h.12
VII
IX
XII
C VII
½C V
X
h.12
VII

IX
VII
X
h.12
VII
IX
VII

V
VII
½C V
VII
V

V
IV
VII
h.12
VII
V
IV
VII

C II
h.12
VII
h.12
V
XI
h.12
IX VII
½C V
IV
V
II
VII
VIII
VII

C II
½C VII
IV
h.12
VII
IX
h.12
II
IV
V
V
VII
V
IV

D.C. al ⊕, then Coda

VII
IX
Rall.
VII
Coda
Rall.
Rall.
Rall.

My Lord Willobie's Welcome Home

Tablature

D.C. al ⊕
then Coda
Coda
Rall.
Rall.

Veri Floris

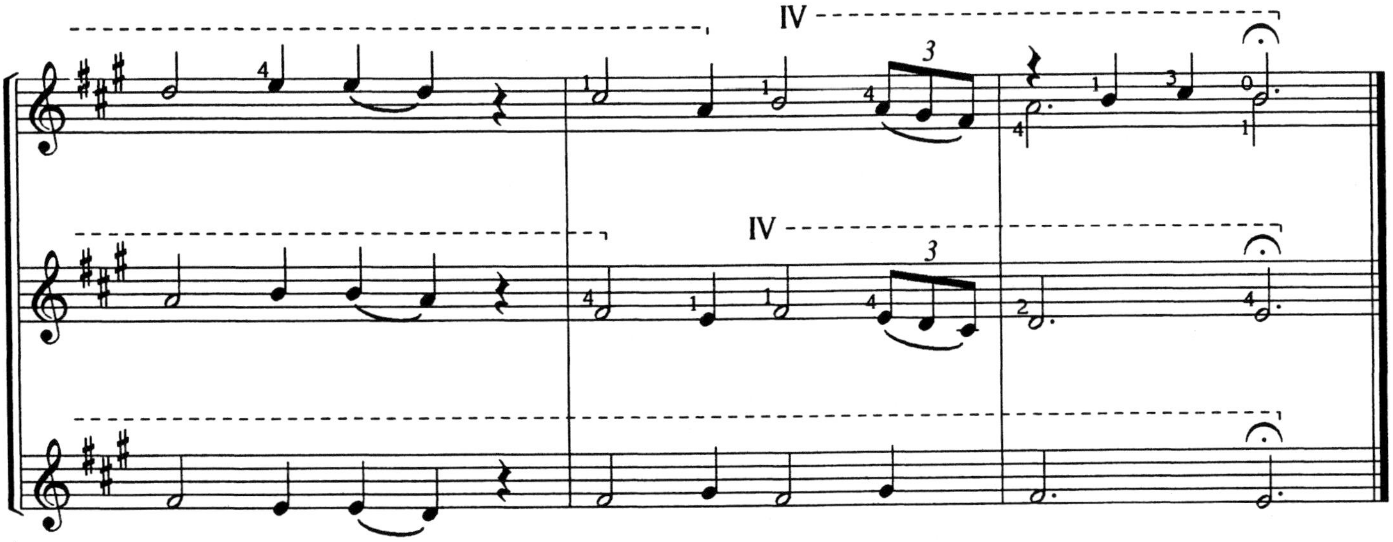

VERI FLORIS

Tablature

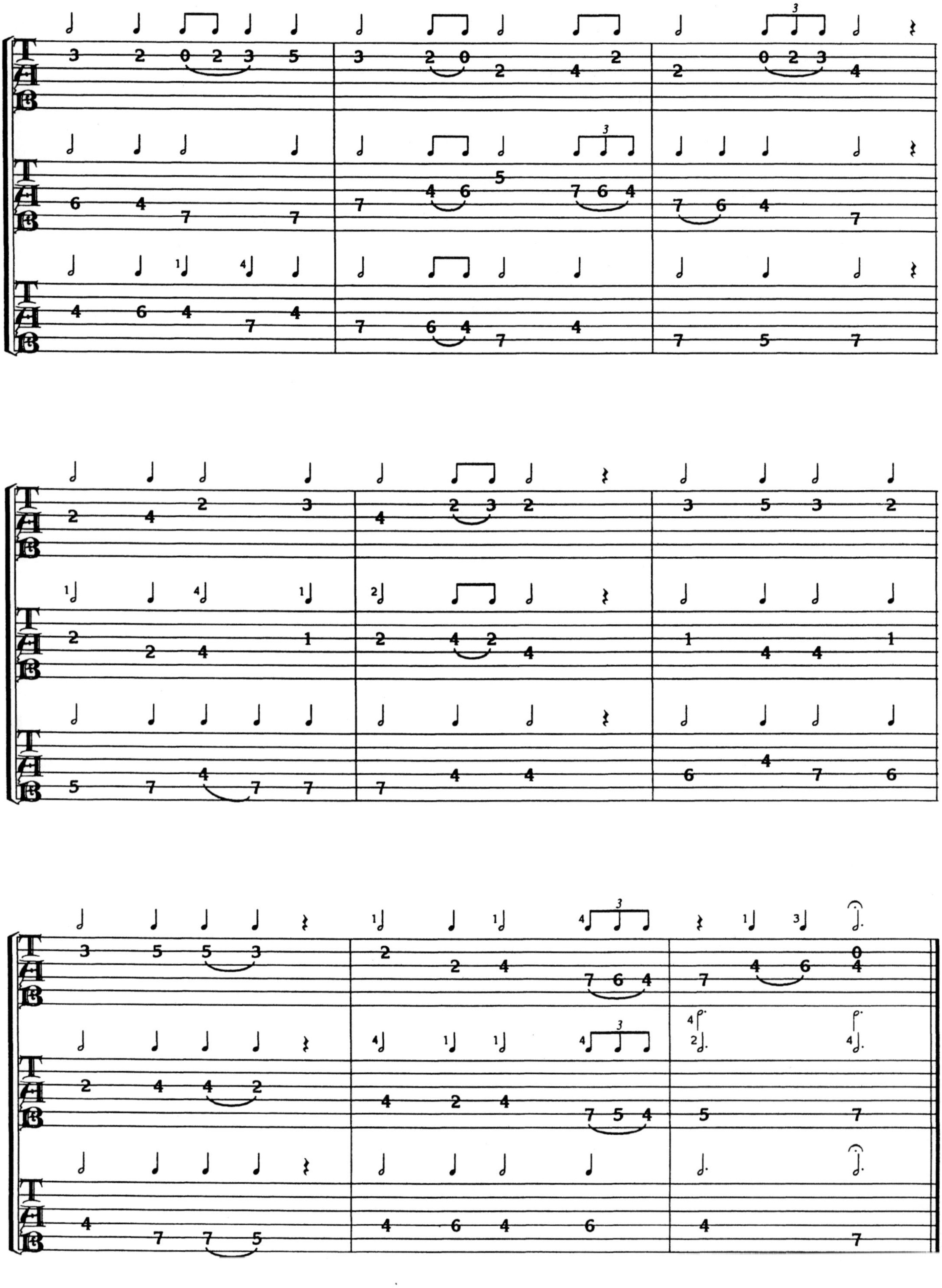

Triple Ballarde

Guillaume de Machaut

Triple Ballarde

Tablature

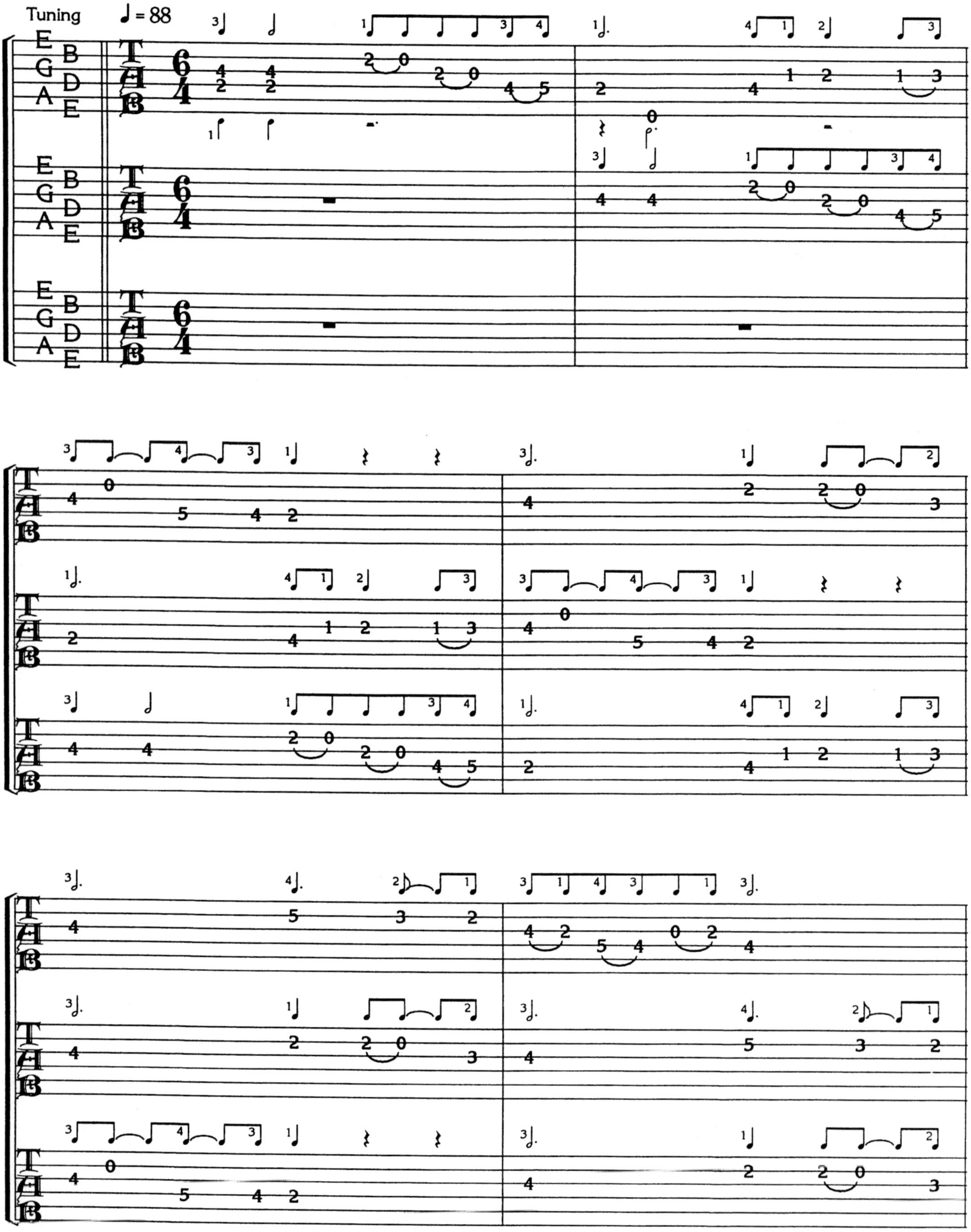

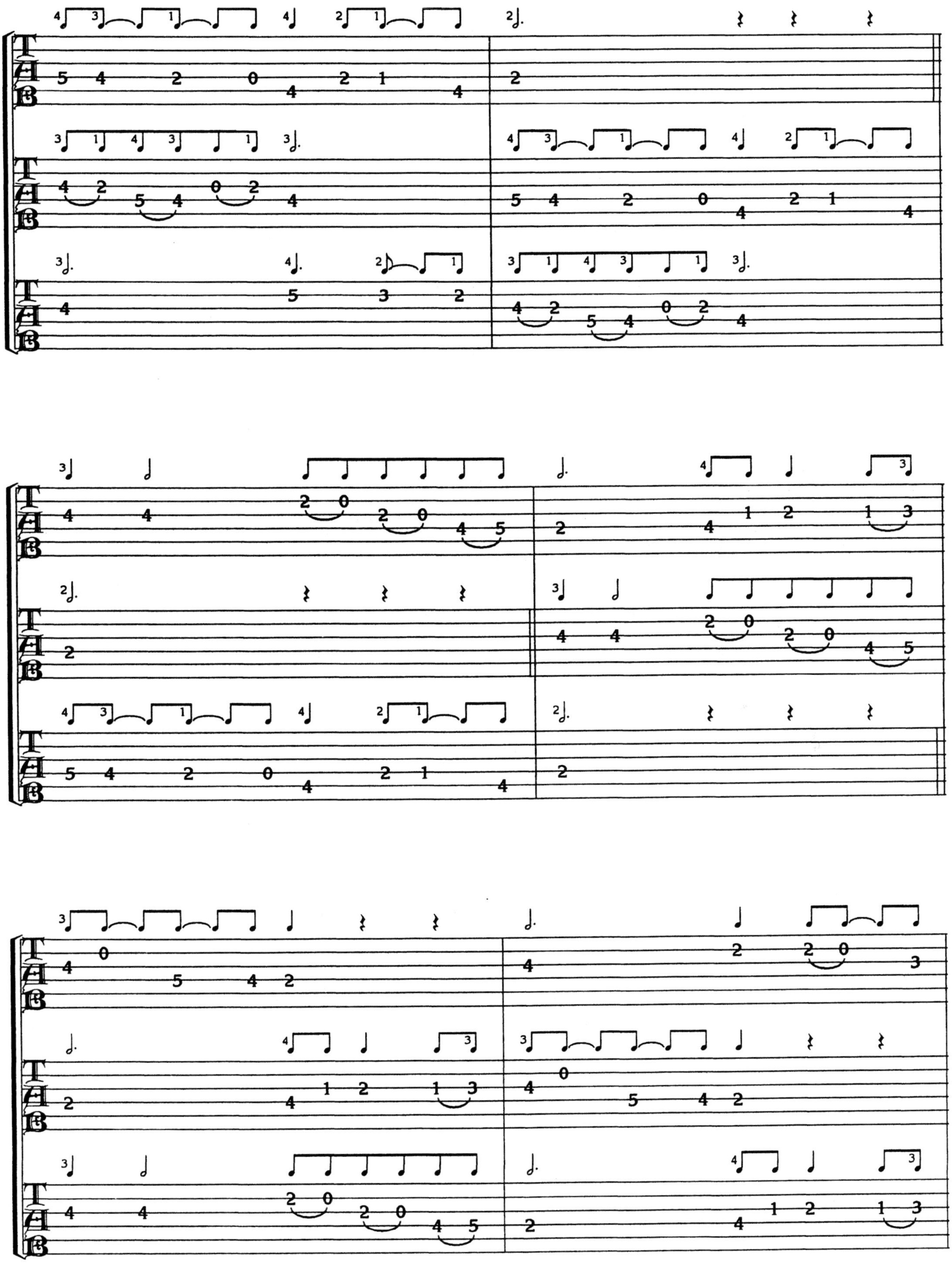

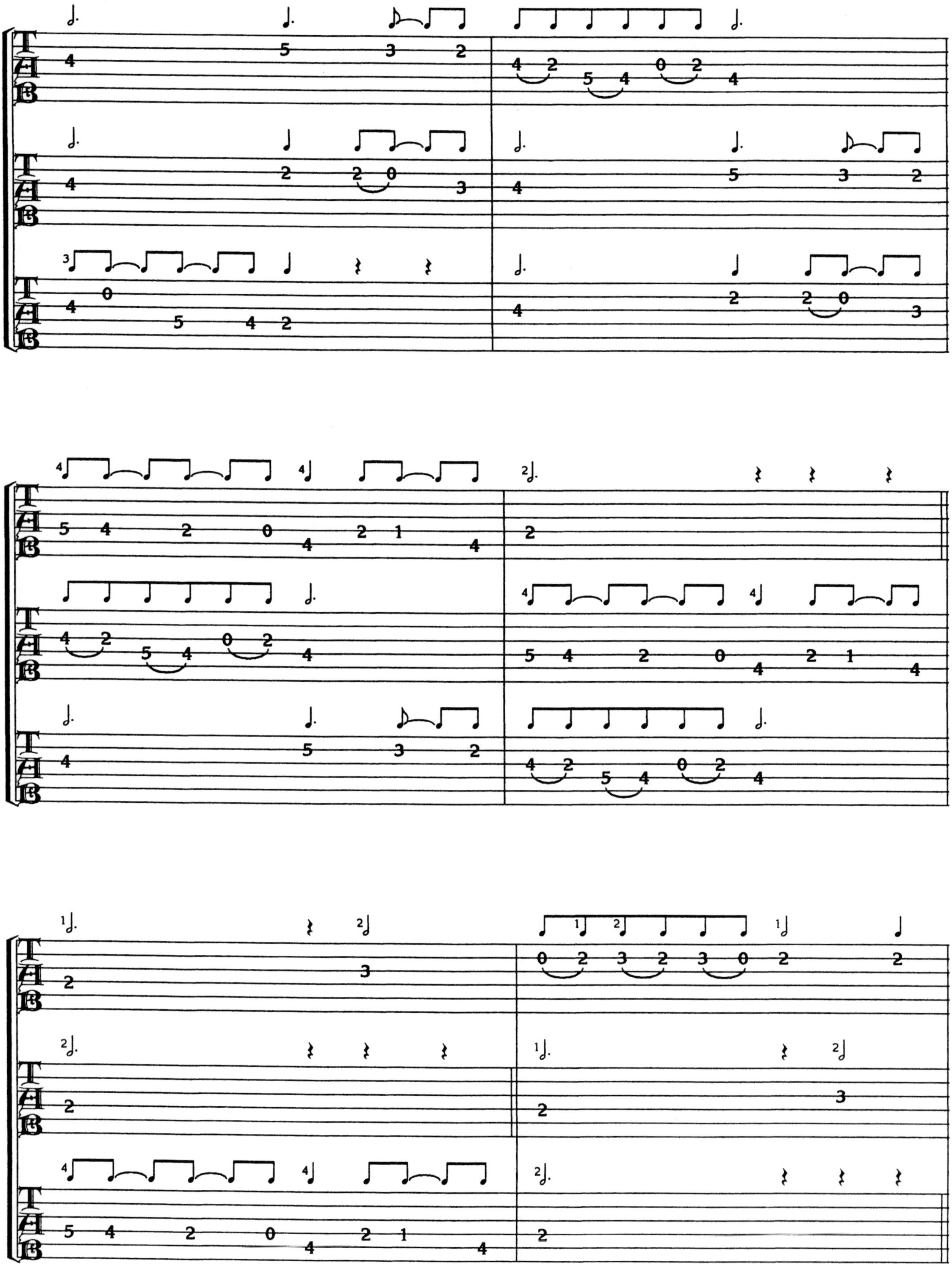

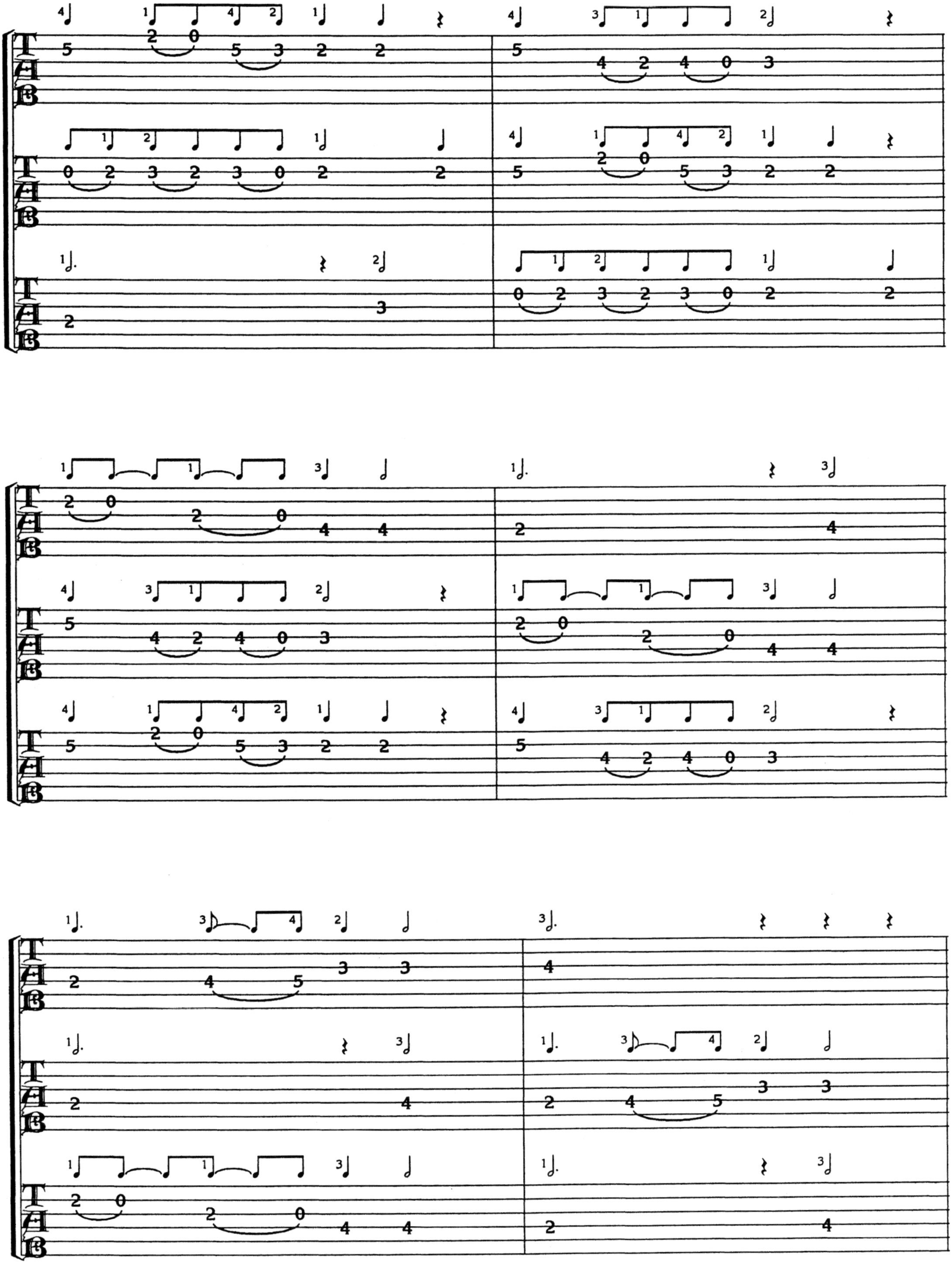

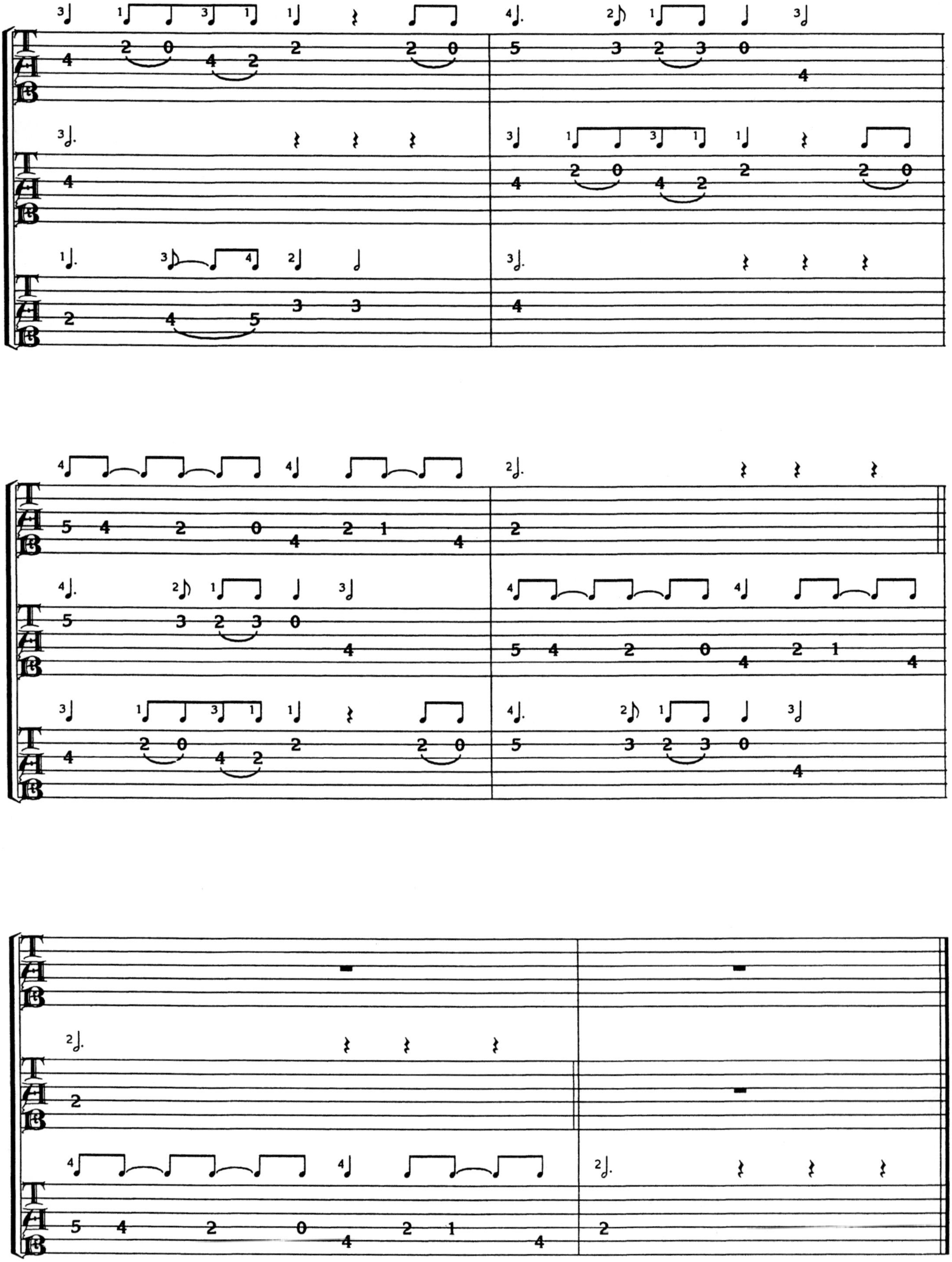

Redford's Meane

John Redford

IX
II
X
II
VII

X
VII
II
V
X
VII
IV
VIII

VII
VIII
II
VII
XII
IX

Redford's Meane

Tablature

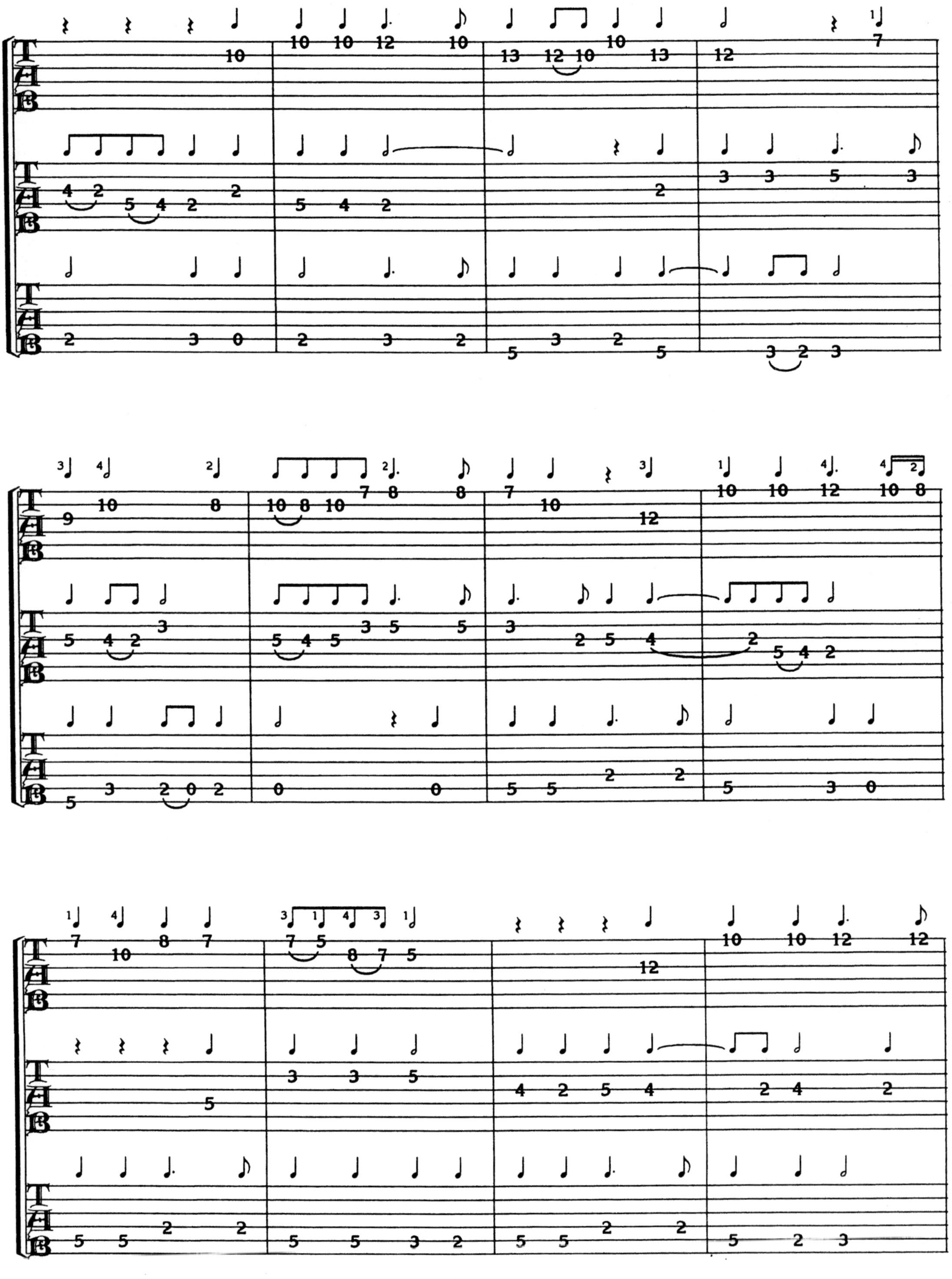

Lachrimae Antiquae

John Dowland

(V)
VII

V
III
V
II
II

VII

V
III
V
II
II
V

VII
½C V
IV

VII
V
IV
V

IX

VII

LACHRIMAE ANTIQUAE
Tablature

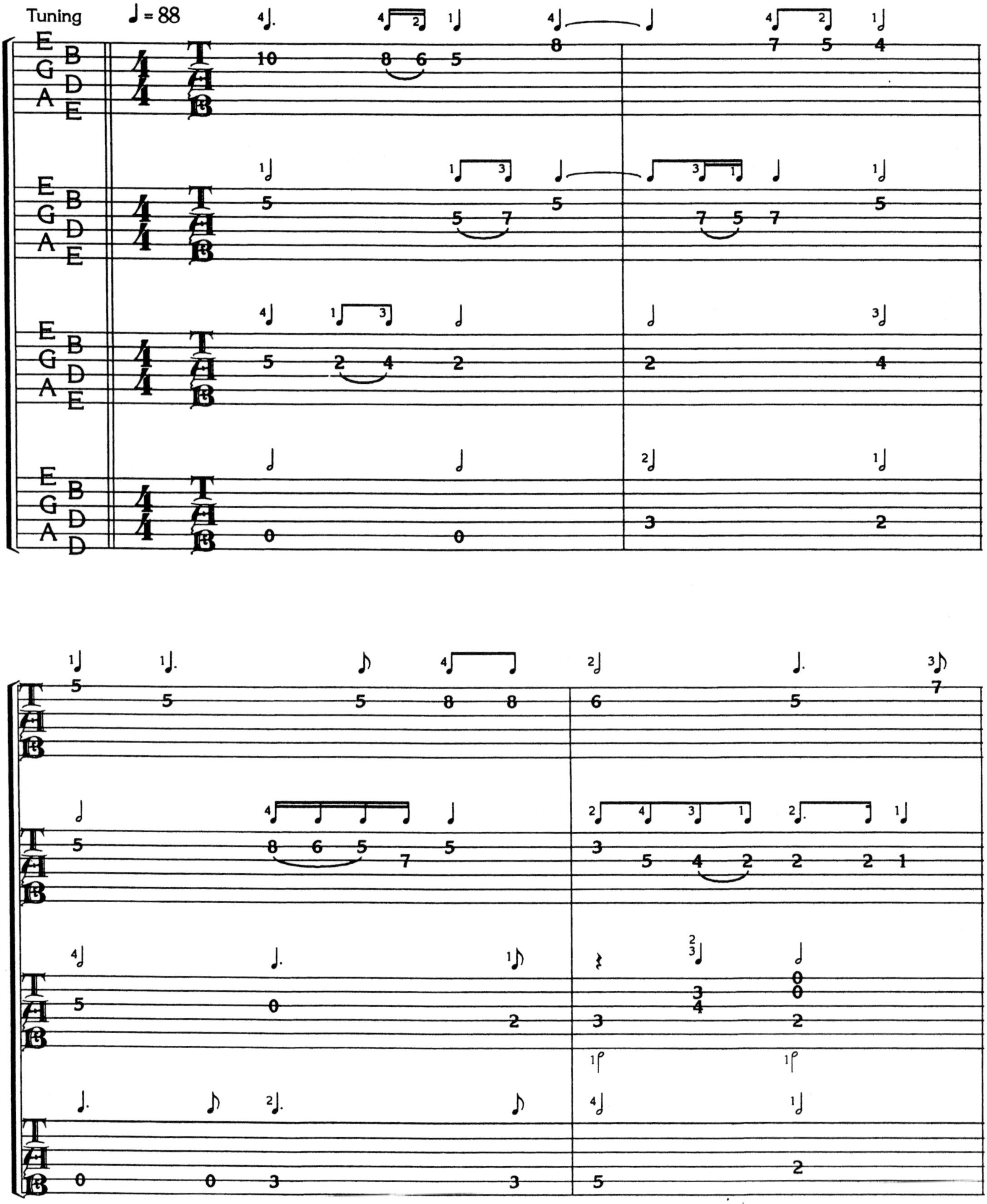

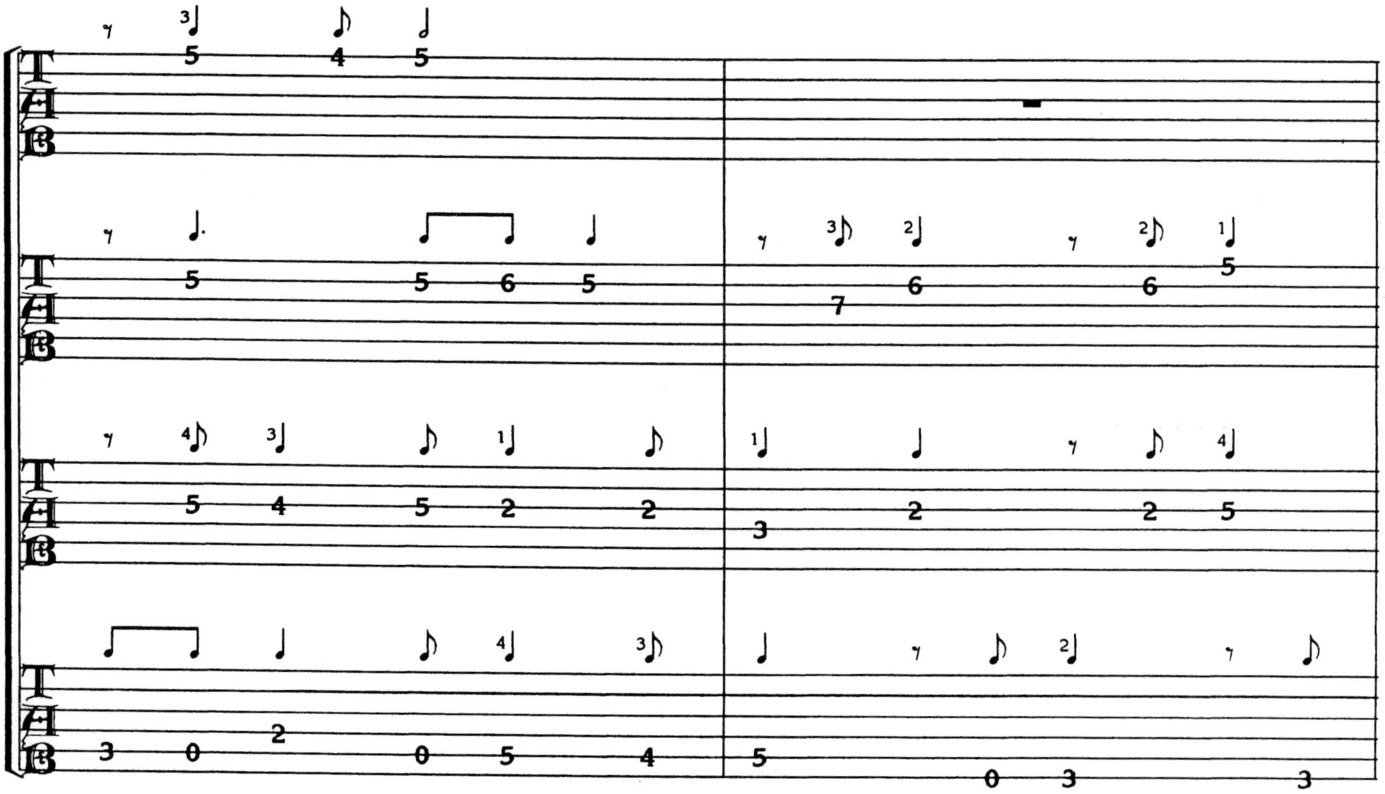

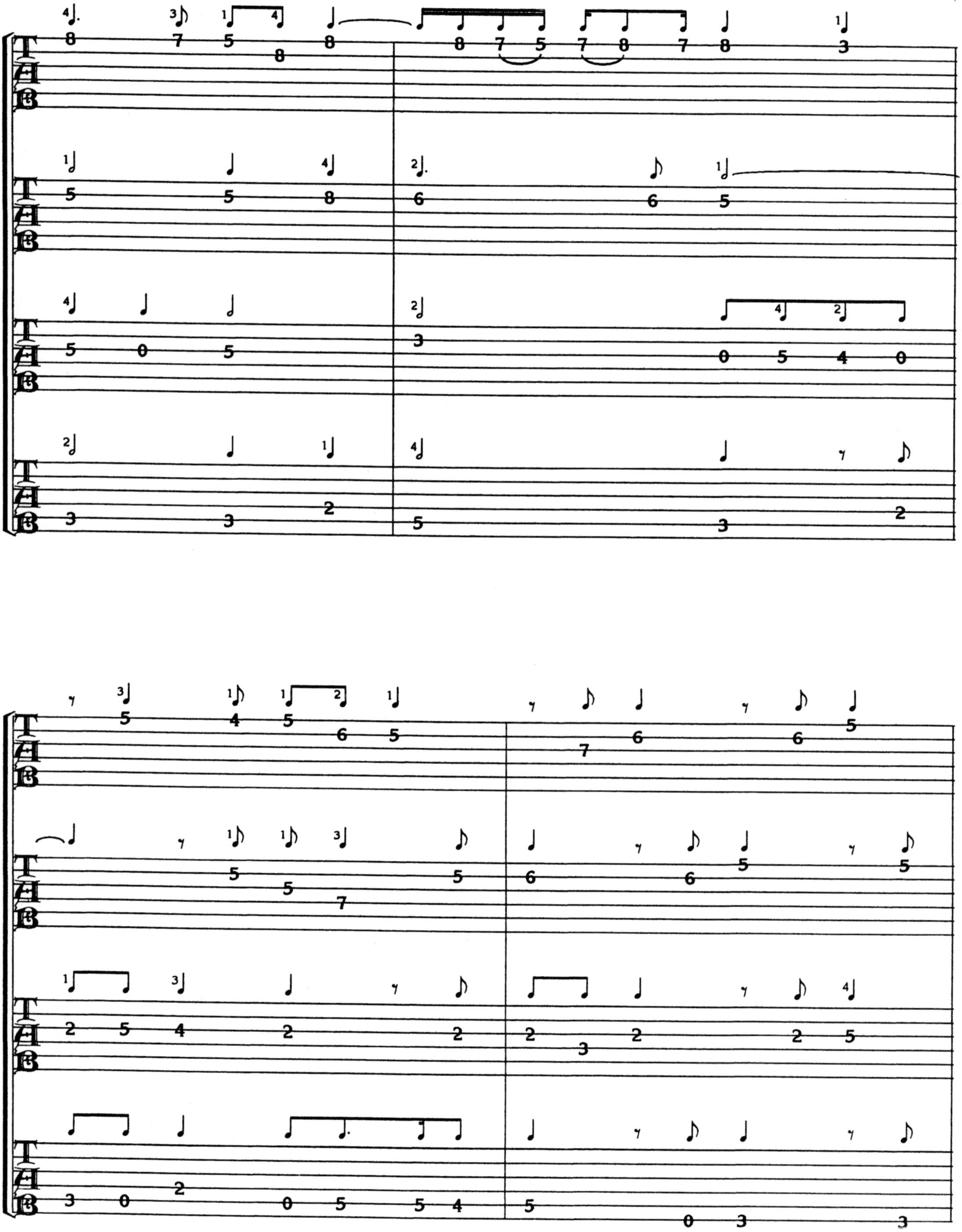

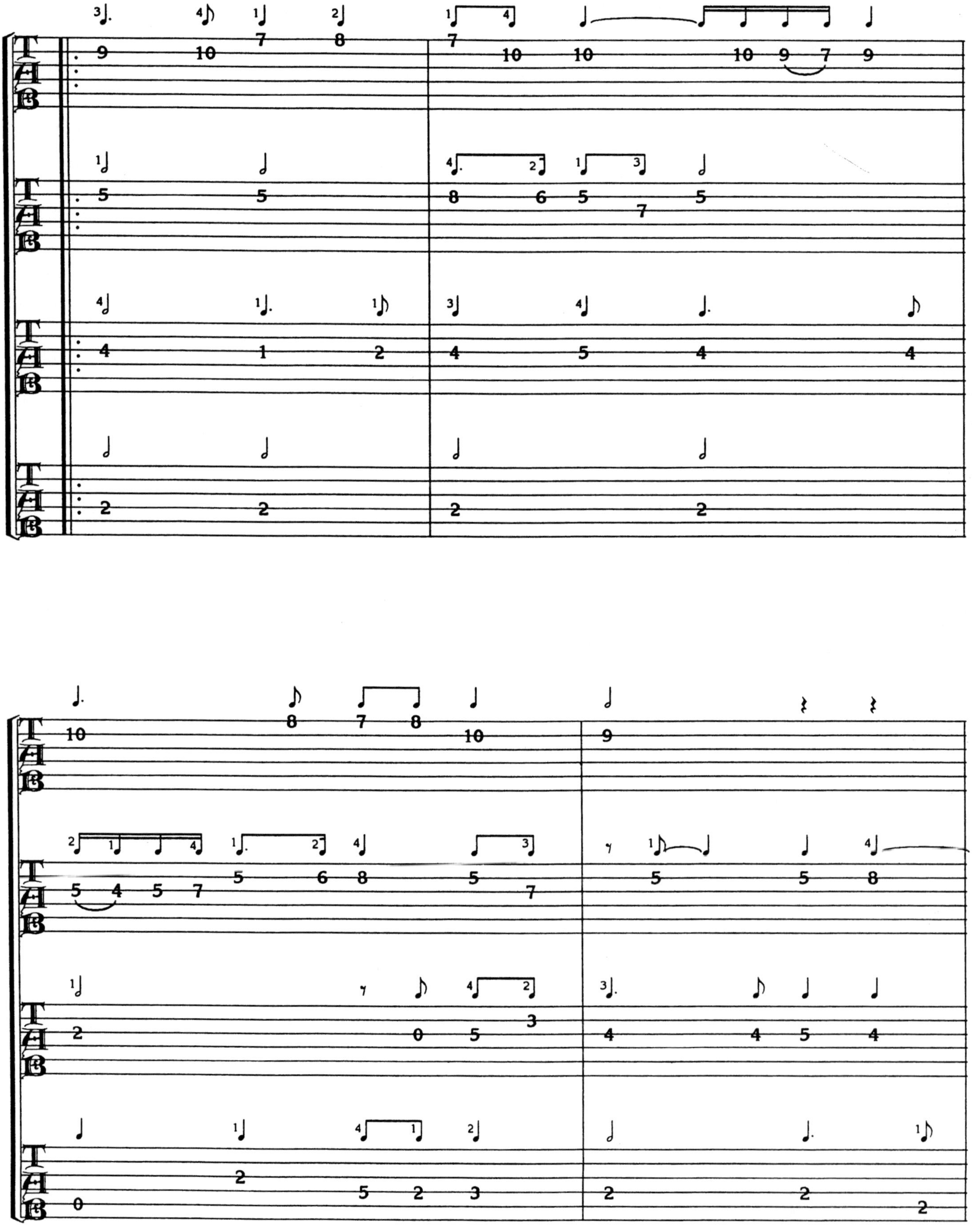

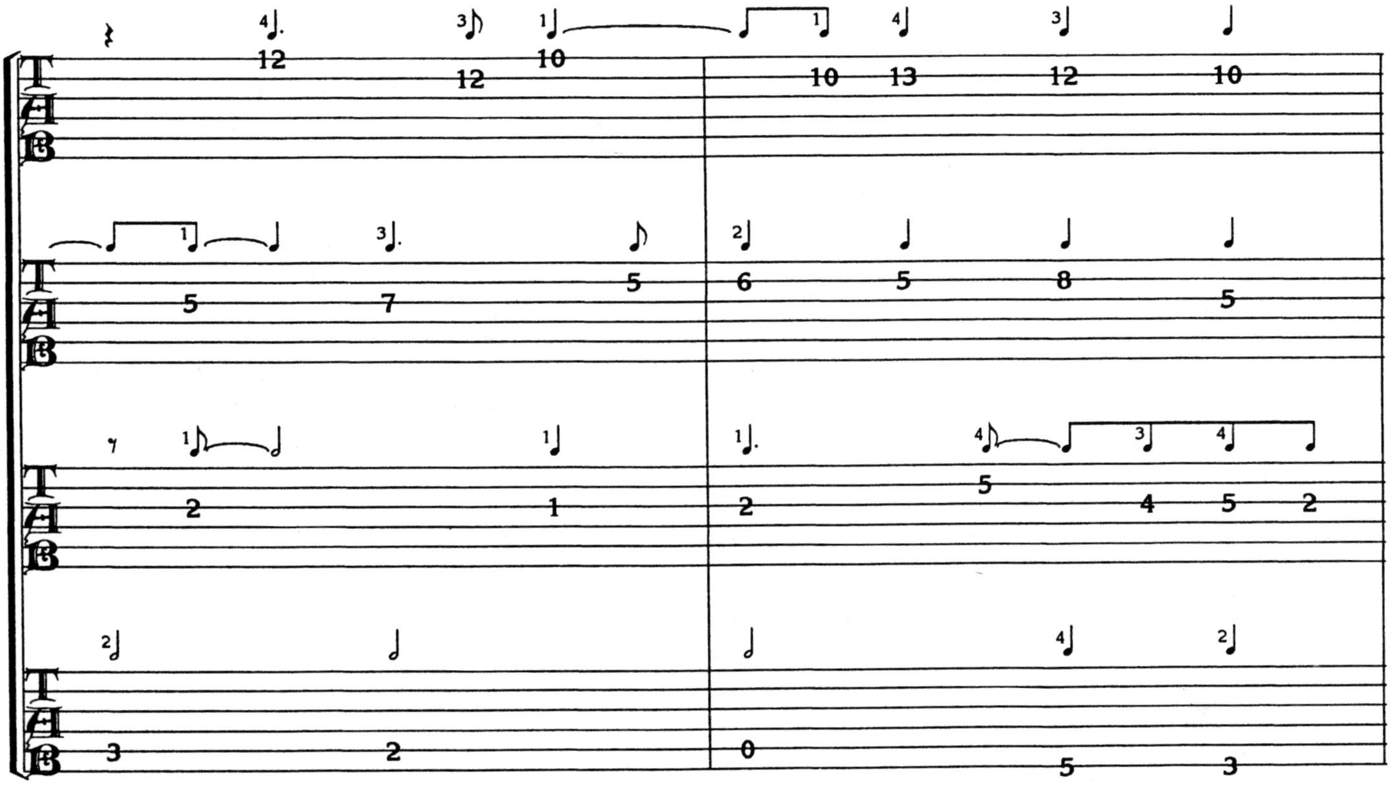

Notes to the Music

1. Lamento di Tristan — Rotta

This pair of fourteenth-century dance tunes from northern Italy are classed as estampies, the earliest known couple dance, each having three sections repeated with first- and second-time endings. They follow the traditional pattern of main dance and after-dance, sharing melodic makeup but contrasting in meter and tempo. The first, with its flowing folk-like melody, is effective both as a slow and rather free lament and as a more evenly-paced processional, whereas the second needs to be considerably more rhythmic. Only the single-line melodies have come down and in setting them on the guitar I have added what I felt to be suitable support lines, mostly open-string drones, in keeping with the mode.

Although both pieces work well on a variety of instruments — the vielle, for example, or the wide-bore low-pitched recorder — possibly the strongest connection is with the metal-strung medieval harp. It is tempting to connect the "Lament" with Sir Tristan who, in the guise of a minstrel harper, set sail from Cornwall to Ireland to claim Isolde. Arthurian romances were very much a stock in trade of the wandering troubadours and would have been well known throughout Europe by the fourteenth century. Music of this type can still be heard even today in some remote mountain areas of northern Italy, the same regions from which early troubadour culture is thought to have emanated. So, the connection is not in fact too intangible.

Certainly the scale-like passages which make up both pieces fall naturally under the fingers on the harp. It would seem appropriate therefore to aim for a touch of harp-like sustain on the guitar by allowing a certain amount of overlap in the phrasing of the melody.

Recordings:

Ulsamer Collegium, *Musique de Danse de la Renaissance.* Archiv Deutsche Grammophon 2533 II.

Medieval and Renaissance Music for the Irish and Medieval Harps - Vièle, Recorders and Tambourin. Turnabout TV43019S.

The Jaye Consort, *Anthology of Medieval Music.* Murray Hill Records, C55051/S.

John Renbourn, *The Lady and the Unicorn.* Shanachie 97022.

2. Saltarello

The Italian "saltarello" appears to have been an early circle dance, possibly the forerunner of the present-day "tarantella." This example, from the fourteenth century, has a fine flowing melody to which I have added some lower lines, mostly in the way of drones supplied by the open strings. The form is essentially two sections repeated with first- and second-time endings. The second section, however, is made up of material from section one preceded by an additional two measures, a device that is taken further in "Saltarello II" (p. 32). The piece can either be played with a steady danceable tempo throughout, in which case the two-bar phrases could be varied (measures 17–18 and 26–27 are suggestions of my own), or else broken up, so that these phrases are left open for out-of-tempo improvisation.

Recording:

John Renbourn, *The Lady and the Unicorn.* Shanachie 97022.

3. Trotto

Like the previous piece this fourteenth-century instrumental dance, from a manuscript in the British Museum, is probably also of Italian origin. The two in fact work well as a pair, "Trotto" following on after the "Saltarello." The jumps in the melodies of both pieces might suggest that they were intended for a blown instrument, possibly a combination of whistle and drum or even the pipes. Again I have added simple lines beneath the melody which tend to reinforce the basic harmonic feel. Rhythmically the piece is bright and up-tempo and is uniformly barred in 6/8 throughout. However, the stresses implied by the harmonic "changes" bring out more interesting underlying phrase lengths, i.e. the triplet groupings of 2 / 2 / 3 / 5 in the first section which would seem unbalanced but nevertheless feel right.

Recordings:

Early Music Quartet, *Secular Music circa 1300.* Telefunken SAWT 9504–AEX.

Ulsamer Collegium, *Musique de Danse de la Renaissance.* Archiv Deutsche Grammophon 2533 I.

John Renbourn, *The Lady and the Unicorn.* Shanachie 97022.

4. Stantipes

"Stantipes," like the Italian "istampita," simply means "estampie." This piece is of a particular type however called a "ductia," which is how it appears in most recorded versions. The ductia, it seems, was rather more formalized than other looser open-ended estampies. It contained between two and four sections each having a set number of beats, contrasting in this respect with the freer-sounding "Saltarello," for example. Here there are three eight-bar sections with the melody in the lower part. The whole is stated twice, each section having a different counter-melody. Although set in two parts it is earlier than the previous single-line dance tunes and comes from the same thirteenth-century English manuscript that contains the well-known vocal canon "Sumer is icumen in." There is a freshness in the feel of the major mode and some delightful interplay between the parts. The whole piece fits almost entirely within a single left-hand position, and the aim is to bring out the independence of the lines while maintaining a light swinging dance tempo.

Recordings:

Medieval and Renaissance Music for the Irish and Medieval Harps - Vièle, Recorders and Tambourin. Turnabout TV43019S.

Ricercare Ensemble of Old Instruments, Zurich, *Estampies, Basse Danses, Pavanes.* Oryx 709.

Musica Reservata, *Medieval Music and Songs of the Troubadours.* Everest 3270.

Studio der Frühen Musik, director Thomas Binkley, *Music des Mittelalters.* Telefunken 653412.

5. The English Dance

A fine multi-sectional estampie thought to date from the middle of the thirteenth century. The original is written on a leaf of parchment that forms the cover to a manuscript of the time of Edward the Confessor. A facsimile is to be found in J. Stainer's

Early Bodleian Music, Volume I. Like "Stantipes" there is a pleasant freshness here in the use of the major mode. The general outline of the tune and some of the repeat figures suggest that it might have been played on a bowed instrument such as the fidel. Although only the single-line melody is given I have added simple tonic and dominant drones, which seem in keeping with the overall feel.

Recordings:

Studio der Frühen Musik, director Thomas Binkley, *Music des Mittelalters*. Telefunken 653412.

The Jaye Consort, *Anthology of Medieval Music*. Murray Hill Records, C55051/S.

John Renbourn, *The Black Balloon*. Shanachie 97009.

6. Saltarello

Literally meaning a "little hop," the "saltarello" was a popular Italian dance from at least the fourteenth century, which is when this version was notated. The music suggests that the dance must have been pretty energetic. Arbeau mentioned later that in this dance the feet were kept close to the ground so that the steps could be executed faster. This is an interesting piece in that it is a variation on the short symmetrical sections common to the estampie. Here an extra measure is added to the second and fourth sections while the endings remain the same. This helps to obscure the sectional divisions and creates something of a accumulative effect. The melody, beneath which I have added some low drones, should fall nicely under the fingers and roll off the fingerboard at a fast but danceable tempo.

Recording:

John Renbourn, *The Nine Maidens*. Flying Fish FF378.

7. Gittern Pavan

This is one of a number of settings for plucked instruments in the *Mulliner Book*, a collection made up largely of English keyboard pieces from the fifteen hundreds. The little gittern would have been light and bright sounding with four double-string courses tuned d g b e', as per the top strings of the modern guitar, and played either with a quill or fingerstyle. The pavan, most stately of the court dances, might well have been taken somewhat faster as an instrumental solo. The short piece is full of character with a subtle interplay between major and minor, arresting harmonic shifts — D major to B flat for example — and the juxtaposition of block chords and florid single-line passages. Notice too the relationship of the lines at measures three and four, indicative of a fingerstyle approach and curiously close to some contemporary folk guitar patterns.

8. Gipsy Dance and Jews' Dance

"Der Zeunertanz" and "Judentanz" are by Hans Neusiedler, a lute player from Nuremberg whose output included a series of books, made up largely of dance tunes, published between 1536 and 1549. These two work well as a pair although each is self-contained and has the form of main dance and after-dance, in which the meter changes from two to three but the overall tempo remains the same. Neusiedler appears to have been more of a teacher than a traveling player and his pieces are generally dependable rather than brilliant. The "Jews' Dance" however would seem to be quite outstanding for the time. The treble line is, for the most part, in a key a semitone apart from that of the bass, resulting in some daring dissonances. It has been commented upon variously as a curious piece of musical satire and as a remarkably early example of bi-tonality. What is also curious is the fact that such innovative elements are conspicuously absent from the remainder of his work. Although it seems a shame to suggest it, there is a possible explanation. Neusiedler chose to write down his pieces in tablature rather than staff notation, which means that while the positions on the fingerboard are clear the actual pitches depend on how the instrument is tuned. At the time there were a good many lute tunings in common use that we know of and quite possibly others that have not survived. Anyway, by making one slight adjustment in the tuning, that of raising the top string by a semitone, the whole piece is transformed. All traces of bi-tonality evaporate and it falls neatly into line with the rest of the pieces. However, we cannot be absolutely certain. Both ways have been committed to record, and so for good measure I have included the two here.

Recordings:

Ricercare Ensemble of Old Instruments, Zurich, *Estampies, Basse Danses, Pavanes*. Oryx 709.

Konrad Ragossnig, lute, *Musique de Dance de la Renaissance*. Archiv Deutsche Grammophon 2533 III.

Julian Bream, lute, *Lute Music from the Royal Courts of Music*. RCA SB–6698.

The John Renbourn Group, *A Maid in Bedlam*. Shanachie 79004

9. Fantasia que contrahaze la harpa en la manera de Luduvico

This is a rather free, and generally most unorthodox interpretation of one of the outstanding pieces from the Spanish vihuela repertoire of the mid-fifteen hundreds. It takes so many liberties that I feel I must point out that the original by Alonso Mudarra is not only very well established but safe and sound in Emilio Pujol's *Hispanæ Citaræ Ars Viva*. Mudarra set out to recreate the style of the harp player Luduvico, who must have been a performer of some repute. The piece is undoubtedly wonderful as it stands, however I found it hard to resist seeing if I could make it even more harp-like, by avoiding barre positions wherever possible and arranging florid passages so that stopped strings held over against open strings. The resulting arrangement, in one of the old parlor guitar tunings, is no more difficult than the authentic one, and should sound effective played with a capo at the third fret. Towards the close there is a striking passage in which the relationship between the ascending bass figures and the treble patterns results in a number of dissonances. Possibly this was an effect that Luduvico was noted for, but Mudarra must have felt that a word of explanation was necessary, as he added the footnote: "Des de aqui fasta acerca hel final hay algunas falsas: taniendose bien no parecen mal." — "From here to the end are some dissonances: played well they will not sound bad."

Recording:

Julian Bream, lute, *Lute Music from the Royal Courts of Music*. RCA SB–6698.

10. Se Lo M'Accorgo

The authorship of this attractive Renaissance Italian lute piece is uncertain. It has been tentatively linked to the Florentine composer Vincenzo Galilei, father of the astronomer Galileo. The old Florentine language is certainly used for the title which can be translated as "Had I But Known." The piece opens on the subdominant before finally settling on the home key and bears comparison with "The Irish Ho-Hoane" in this respect. The descending imitative passages in the second part seem to reflect the title and transfer well onto the guitar.

Recording:
Davey Graham, *The Complete Guitarist.*
Kicking Mule SNKF 138.

11 & 12. Bransle Gay and Bransle de Bourgogne

These are both from the *Danseries* of Claude Gervaise, comprehensive collections of dance tunes set in four and five parts, published in the mid-fifteen hundreds. Frequently drawing on folk material, Gervaise produced working arrangements for the Renaissance band which are often catchy as well as practical. The bransle was, I believe, a French country dance originally — taking its name from "branler" meaning to gyrate. The dance enjoyed widespread popularity, catching on in England where it became known as the "brawl" and continuing as a firm favorite in Scotland. Many of the pieces in the *Danseries* are still colored by the old modes — "Bransle Gay," in section one, has a mixolydian feel before settling on d–dorian. "Bransle de Bourgogne" begins squarely in D major but shifts to e–dorian after eight bars. This piece too has some subtle touches — the attractive figure at measures thirteen and fourteen, for example, and the choice of E minor for the final close rather than a return to D major.

Recordings:
Medieval and Renaissance Music for the Irish and Medieval Harps - Vièle, Recorders and Tambourin.
Turnabout TV43019S.
John Renbourn, *The Lady and the Unicorn.* Shanachie 97022.

13. The Irish Ho-Hoane

One of a number of attractive short anonymous keyboard pieces in the *Fitzwilliam Virginal Book.* "Ho-Hoane" is evidently a variation of "Och-One," the Irish lament for the dead. The arrangement is rather plain but works well that way. However, there is certainly room for melodic ornamentation on the repeats.

14. Bandora Lullaby

The bandora, together with the orpharion, were metal-strung plucked instruments that shared the solo repertoire of the lute as well as being consort instruments. The larger bandora had seven courses tuned G c d g c' e' a', the top five courses being equivalent to the modern guitar tuning, having the interval of a third between strings two and three. A small amount of specific bandora music has survived. One source is William Barley's *New Book of Tablature* of 1596. This charming piece is by the Elizabethan composer Anthony Holborne. I have had to alter a few notes here and there to suit the guitar. The original can be found in *The Complete Works of Anthony Holborne — Music for Lute and Bandora.* (Harvard Publications in Music.)

15. Pavanne d'Espagne

This piece, known in England as the "Spanish Pavin," enjoyed immense popularity throughout the reigns of Queen Elizabeth and James I. Brisker in tempo, its more ornate dance steps set it apart from the conventional stately pavan. The setting here is by French lutenist Nicholas Vallet, from *Le Secret Des Muses,* Book II, 1616. I have been tempted to include three pieces by Vallet. The part writing is sparse but with strong clear lines which transpose well onto the guitar. By using the tuning C G c g c' f', which extends the normal range of the guitar by a fourth, it is possible to duplicate the lute parts and retain the distinction between bass and treble. Other settings for the lute are included in William Ballet's *Lute Book* and Thomas Robinson's *Schoole of Musicke.* An arrangement for keyboard by Dr. John Bull is to be found in the *Fitzwilliam Virginal Book.*

16. Bouree I and Bouree II

Also from Nicholas Vallet's *Le Secret Des Muses,* Book II, a collection of popular songs and dance tunes arranged for solo lute. Both these pieces appeared earlier in the *Terpsichore* of Michael Praetorius and later, as variants, in Playford's *The English Dancing Master.*

Recordings:
Eugene M. Dombois, lute, *Michael Praetorius Terpsichore 1612.* EMI CO63–30–117.
James Tyler, *Music of the Renaissance Virtuoso.* Saga 5438.
John Renbourn, *The Black Balloon.* Shanachie 97009.

17. Mal Sims

This piece has come down to us in a number of settings. It seems likely to have been a popular song and was known as the "English Echo" presumably from the imitative passages or chorus. Nicholas Vallet included a "Malsimmes, Bal Anglais" for solo lute in *Le Secret Des Muses,* Book I, 1615, and yet another version in his second collection. There is also a keyboard setting by Giles Farnaby in the *Fitzwilliam Virginal Book.*

18. The Earle of Salisbury

The stately pavan was the most enduring of the court dances. The name is said to derive from "Padoana," the ancient dance of Padua, and the earliest noted version is from the beginning of the fifteen hundreds. This fine keyboard pavan is by one of the outstanding English composers of the sixteenth century, William Byrd. Byrd included the piece in his collection *Parthenia* published in 1611, the title page of which bears the inscription "the first musicke that was ever printed for the virginalls." In spite of some necessary reductions in the outlay of the parts the piece as a whole, I think, transfers successfully onto the guitar.

Recording:
John Renbourn, *Sir John Alot.* Shanachie 97021.

19. Courante

Robert Ballard, lutenist to the French court, was a contemporary of Nicholas Vallet. His exceptional arrangements are contained in two collections of *Diverses Pièces Mises sur le Luth,* and include a number of pieces that appeared later in

Vallet's *Le Secret Des Muses.* The "Courante" is listed as number two in the *Premier Livre* of 1611. As one of the set dances from the sixteenth century the triple-time courante provided a light contrast to the solemn pavan. Ballard's arrangement was originally notated in 6/4 but I have it here in 3/4 as per conventional practice. However, although rather easier to read perhaps, the overall rhythmic feel is often across the whole two bars, particularly so towards the end variations.

20. The Moon Shines Bright

Strictly speaking, I suppose, this one is a little late for the Renaissance. But then again such things came later in some places and may still be overdue in others. This is a set of variations based on a traditional English carol sometimes called the "Old Wait's Carol," but probably more widely known as the "Bellman's Song," as it commonly appeared in old broadsides. I have stuck to the basic harmonic scheme throughout each of the variations, with the melody appearing variously in the treble, middle, and bass parts. Three quite separate versions of the tune can be found in *The Oxford Book of Carols.*

Recording:
John Renbourn, *The Black Balloon.* Shanachie 97009.

21. Toy for Two Lutes

The English musician Thomas Robinson is mainly known for his *Schoole of Musicke* published in 1603. Together with instructions in the art of lute playing the book contains a fine selection of pieces, mostly for solo lute, with settings of the "Spanish Pavan" and "Lord Willobie's Welcome Home." Also included are a number of attractive and inventive duets, of which this is one. The "Toy," like the "Nothynge" and the "Puff," was usually a light piece that fell outside the conventions of the larger set forms.

Recordings:
Diana Poulton, *Music of Shakespeare's Time.* HMV CLP1634.
John Renbourn, *The Hermit.* Shanachie 97041.

22. Westron Wynde

"Westron Wynde" was one of the well-known secular songs used as the cantus firmus for early English settings of the mass, including those of Tavener, Tye and Shepherd. The melody that forms the basis of this arrangement is from the sixteenth century and consequently a later version. The two sections are to be played consecutively with the first section entirely in natural harmonics. The only remaining verse to the song is:

"Westron Wynde, when wilt thou blow,
And the smalle rain down can rain,
Christ that my love was in my arms
And I in my bed agayne."

Recording:
John Renbourn, *The Lady and the Unicorn.* Shanachie 97022.

23. Alman

Most probably of German origin, this dance may have been introduced into England from France. The earliest mention in print in England was in 1521, the word "Allemande" being used in reference to the French style of the basse danse. The Italians called the dance "Saltarello tedesco," that is, in the German style. As the "Alman," "Almayne" and "Almon," it enjoyed popularity throughout the reign of Elizabeth I, taking its place alongside the sarabande and courante as one of the set dances. A good many keyboard versions have survived by English composers. This anonymous Alman was included in the *Fitzwilliam Virginal Book* together with arrangements by Bull, Johnson and Byrd. Although uncredited it is a fine, well-crafted piece and bears comparison with the better-known "My Lord Willobie's Welcome Home," which follows.

24. My Lord Willobie's Welcome Home

This appears to have been a very well-known Elizabethan piece. There are settings for solo lute by Thomas Robinson and Nicholas Vallet (as Soet Robbert), also by Dowland, with a second part added anonymously, and an arrangement by Byrd in the *Fitzwilliam Virginal Book* (as "Rowland"). It seems that the tune was made popular by Will Kemp and his players, who accompanied Robert Dudley, Earl of Leicester, to the Netherlands. When Dudley was disgraced and recalled he was succeeded by Lord Willoughby and, in the hope of finding a new patron, Kemp renamed the piece in his honor.

Recordings:
Julian Bream, lute, *Julian Bream in Concert.*
RCA Victor RB 6646.
John Renbourn, *The Hermit.* Shanachie 97041.

25. Veri Floris

A French three-part conductus from the Notre Dame School of the thirteenth century. This setting of a metrical poem, in what was the new style, appears to have been highly thought of at the time as it has been found in at least nine separate manuscripts. The main melody is the lowest part with the upper parts in similar rhythm so that vertical, or chordal, harmonies arise. A translation of the words would be:

"Under the figure of the true flower which the pure root produced, the loving devotion of our clergy has made a mystical flower, constructing an allegorical meaning beyond the usage from the nature of a flower."

Recording:
John Renbourn, *The Lady and the Unicorn.* Shanachie 97022.

26. Triple Ballarde

Guillaume de Machaut was a churchman, poet and leading French composer of the early fourteenth century. His compositions ranged from catchy arrangements of folk tunes to the full-scale setting of the mass — "La Messe de Nostre Dame" of 1300, being a landmark in western music. A famous and no doubt romantic figure, Machaut enjoyed the privilege of having his works preserved in luxurious illustrated volumes during his lifetime. This three-part canonic ballade, originally for voices set to the texts of "Sans cuer," "Amis dolens," and "Dame par vous," is also effective as an instrumental piece — the single-line melody alone is outstanding. The accepted interpretation as a canon is with the parts entering at a distance of one bar, as notated here. However, Machaut was often deliberately cryptic in the construction of his pieces, and it is possible that there are more interpretations than one. The piece also works having the entries at measures three and five, that is two bars apart. Both ways result in exposed dissonances with the minor seventh sounding above the major seventh. These false relations continued as a cadential convention into the sixteen hundreds — similar passages will be seen in the pieces of Redford and Dowland. An interesting variation is to have the entries at measures four and five, which creates a combination of the two and softens the dissonances.

Recordings:

Guillaume de Machaut "La Messe de Notre Dame — 10 Weltliche Werke."
Archiv Deutsche Grammophon 14063.

John Renbourn, *The Lady and the Unicorn.* Shanachie 97022.

27. Redford's Meane

John Redford is considered to be among the most outstanding of the English keyboard composers before the virginalists. In the early fifteen hundreds he held the position of organist and choirmaster at St. Paul's Cathedral, where the service included sections that called for exchanges between organ and choir. Extemporization based on plainsong, or "breaking the plainsong," would still have been common practice at that time, and Redford was singled out by Thomas Morley at the end of the century, after a period of considerable musical development, as being a master of that art. The majority of Redford's compositions to have survived are contained in the *Mulliner Book.* These include a number of excellent three-part Meanes in which the "meane," or middle part, is passed between the two hands and is notated in black ink to separate it from the overall texture.

28. Lachrimae Antiquae

John Dowland is the most celebrated of the lutenist songwriters of the Elizabethan age. Long claimed by the English, his place of birth remains uncertain, while the origins of his surname and his own written references to "my fellow countrymen" could equally well connect him with Ireland. He certainly chose to remain out of England, traveling in France, Germany and Italy, with an eight-year stay in Denmark at the court of Christian IV. Dowland seems to have been reluctant to publish his own pieces but was critical of editions that contained unauthorized versions. The "Lachrimae Pavan," among his most famous lute solos, did not appear in print until 1605, and then in a collection that contained seven settings for lute and five viols. This is an arrangement of the first, the "Lachrimae Antiquae," and I have drawn on a combination of lute and viol parts in arriving at this setting for four guitars.

Recordings:

Julian Bream, lute, *Julian Bream plays Dowland.* EMI.

Music of Shakespeare's Time. HMV CLP 1634.